SHOPTALK

In the 1990s Philip Roth won America's four major literary awards in succession: the National Book Critics Circle Award for *Patrimony* (1991), the PEN/Faulkner Award for *Operation Shylock* (1993), the National Book Award for *Sabbath's Theater* (1995), and the Pulitzer Prize in fiction for *American Pastoral* (1997). He won the Ambassador Book Award of the English-Speaking Union for *I Married a Communist* (1998); in the same year he received the National Medal of Arts at the White House. Previously, he won the National Book Critics Circle Award for *The Counterlife* (1986) and the National Book Award for his first book, *Goodbye Columbus* (1959). In 2000 he published *The Human Stain*, concluding a trilogy that depicts the ideological ethos of post-war America. For *The Human Stain* Roth received his second PEN/Faulkner Award as well as the W.H. Smith Literary Award in Britain. In 2001 he received the highest award of the American Academy of Arts and Letters: the Gold Medal in fiction, given every six years 'for the entire work of the recipient'. His latest novel is *The Dying Animal*.

ALSO BY PHILIP ROTH

Philip Roth

SHOP TALK

A Writer and His Colleagues
and Their Work

VINTAGE

Published by Vintage 2002

2 4 6 8 10 9 7 5 3 1

First published in Great Britain by
Jonathan Cape 2001

Vintage
Random House, 20 Vauxhall Bridge Road,
London SW1V 2SA

Random House Australia (Pty) Limited
20 Alfred Street, Milsons Point, Sydney
New South Wales 2061, Australia

Random House New Zealand Limited
18 Poland Road, Glenfield,
Auckland 10, New Zealand

Random House (Pty) Limited
Endulini, 5A Jubilee Road, Parktown 2193,
South Africa

The Random House Group Limited Reg. No. 954009
www.randomhouse.co.uk

A CIP catalogue record for this book
is available from the British Library

ISBN 0 099 42843 1

Papers used by Random House are natural, recyclable
products made from wood grown in sustainable forests.
The manufacturing processes conform to the environ-
mental regulations of the country of origin

Printed and bound in Great Britain by
Bookmarque Ltd, Croydon, Surrey

FOR MY FRIEND C.H. HUVELLE
1916–2000

Contents

Shop Talk

Primo Levi

[1986]

O N THE FRIDAY in September 1986 that I arrived in Turin to renew a conversation with Primo Levi that we had begun one afternoon in London the spring before, I asked to be shown around the paint factory where he'd been employed as a research chemist and, afterward, until retirement, as manager. Altogether the company employs fifty people, mainly chemists who work in the laboratories and skilled laborers on the floor of the plant. The production machinery, the row of storage tanks, the laboratory building, the finished product in man-sized containers ready to be shipped, the reprocessing facility that purifies the wastes—all of it is encompassed in four or five acres seven miles from Turin. The machines that are drying resin and blending varnish and pumping off pollutants are never distressingly loud, the yard's acrid odor—the smell, Levi told me, that clung to his clothing for two years after his retirement—is by no means disgusting, and the thirty-yard Dumpster loaded to the brim with the black sludgy residue of the antipolluting process isn't particularly unsightly. It is hardly the world's ugliest industrial environment, but a long way nonetheless from those sentences suffused with mind that are the hallmark of Levi's autobiographical narratives.

However far from the spirit of the prose, the factory is clearly close to his heart; taking in what I could of the noise, the stink, the mosaic of pipes and vats and tanks and dials, I remembered Faussone, the skilled rigger in *The Monkey's Wrench*, saying to Levi, who calls Faussone "my alter ego," "I have to tell you, being around a work site is something I enjoy."

As we walked through the open yard to the laboratory, a simply designed two-story building constructed during Levi's managerial days, he told me, "I have been cut off from the factory for twelve years. This will be an adventure for *me*." He said he believed that nearly everybody once working with him was now retired or dead, and indeed, those few still there whom he ran into seemed to strike him as specters. "It's another ghost," he whispered to me after someone from the central office that had once been his emerged to welcome him back. On our way to the section of the laboratory where raw materials are scrutinized before moving to production, I asked Levi if he could identify the chemical aroma faintly permeating the corridor: I thought it smelled like a hospital corridor. Just fractionally he raised his head and exposed his nostrils to the air. With a smile he told me, "I understand and can analyze it like a dog."

He seemed to me inwardly animated more in the manner of some quicksilver little woodland creature enlivened by the forest's most astute intelligence. Levi is small and slight, though not so delicately built as his unassuming demeanor makes him at first appear, and seemingly as nimble as he must have been at ten. In his body, as in his face, you see—as you don't in most men—the face and the body of the boy that he was. The alertness is nearly palpable, keenness trembling within like his pilot light.

It is not as surprising as one might initially think to find that writers divide like the rest of mankind into two categories: those who listen to you and those who don't. Levi listens, and with his entire face, a precisely modeled face that, tipped with its white chin beard, looks at sixty-seven youthfully Panlike and professorial as well, the face of irrepressible curiosity and of the esteemed *dottore*. I can believe Faussone when he says to Primo Levi early in *The Monkey's Wrench*, "You're quite a guy, making me tell these stories that, except for you, I've never told anybody." It's no wonder that people are always telling him things and that everything is already faithfully recorded before it is written down: when listening he is as focused and as still as a chipmunk spying something unknown from atop a stone wall.

In a large, substantial-looking apartment house built a few years before he was born—indeed the house where he *was* born, for formerly this was the home of his parents—Levi lives with his wife, Lucia; except for his year in Auschwitz and the adventurous months immediately after his liberation, he has lived in this apartment all his life. The building, whose bourgeois solidity has begun slightly to give way to time, is on a wide boulevard of apartment buildings that struck me as the northern Italian counterpart of Manhattan's West End Avenue: a steady stream of auto and bus traffic, trolley cars speeding by on their tracks, but also a column of big chestnut trees stretching all along the narrow islands at either side of the street, and the green hills bordering the city visible from the intersection. The famous arcades at the commercial heart of the city are an unswerving fifteen-minute walk straight through what Levi has called "the obsessive Turin geometry."

The Levis' large apartment is shared, as it has been since the couple met and married after the war, with Primo Levi's mother. She is ninety-one. Levi's ninety-five-year-old mother-in-law lives not far away; in the apartment next door lives his twenty-eight-year-old son, a physicist; and a few streets farther on is his thirty-eight-year-old daughter, a botanist. I don't know of another contemporary writer who has voluntarily remained, over so many decades, intimately entangled and in such direct, unbroken contact with his immediate family, his birthplace, his region, the world of his forebears, and, particularly, the local working environment, which in Turin, the home of Fiat, is largely industrial. Of all the intellectually gifted artists of the twentieth century—and Levi's uniqueness is that he is more the artist-chemist than the chemist-writer—he may well be the most thoroughly adapted to the totality of the life around him. Perhaps in the case of Primo Levi, a life of communal interconnectedness, along with his masterpiece on Auschwitz, constitutes his profoundly spirited response to those who did all they could to sever his every sustained connection and tear him and his kind out of history.

In *The Periodic Table,* beginning with the simplest of sentences a paragraph that describes one of chemistry's most satisfying processes, Levi writes, "Distilling is beautiful." What follows is a distillation too, a reduction to essential points of the lively, wide-ranging conversation we conducted, in English, over the course of a long weekend, mostly behind the door of the quiet study off the entrance foyer to the Levis' apartment. His study is a large, simply furnished room. There is an old flowered sofa and a comfortable easy chair; on the desk is a shrouded word processor; neatly shelved behind the desk are Levi's variously colored notebooks; on shelves all around the room are books in Italian, German, and English. The most evocative object is one of the smallest: an unobtrusively hung sketch of a half-destroyed barbed-wire fence at Auschwitz. Displayed more prominently on the walls are playful constructions skillfully twisted into shape by Levi himself out of insulated copper wire—that is, wire coated with the varnish developed for that purpose in his own laboratory. There is a big wire butterfly, a wire owl, a tiny wire bug, and high on the wall behind the desk are two of the largest constructions: one the wire figure of a bird-warrior armed with a knitting needle and the other, as Levi explained when I couldn't make out what the figure was meant to represent, "a man playing his nose." "A Jew," I suggested. "Yes, yes," he said, laughing, "a Jew, of course."

Roth: In *The Periodic Table*, your book about "the strong and bitter flavor" of your experience as a chemist, you tell about Giulia, your attractive young colleague in a Milan chemical factory in 1942. Giulia explains your "mania about work" by the fact that in your early twenties you are shy with women and don't have a girlfriend. But she was mistaken, I think. Your real mania about work derives from something deeper. Work would seem to be your chief subject, not just in *The Monkey's Wrench* but even in your first book, about your incarceration at Auschwitz.

Arbeit Macht Frei—"Work Makes Freedom"—are the words inscribed by the Nazis over the Auschwitz gate. But work in Auschwitz is a horrifying parody of work, useless and senseless—labor as punishment leading to agonizing death. It's possible to view your entire literary labor as dedicated to restoring to work its humane meaning, reclaiming the word *Arbeit* from the derisive cynicism with which your Auschwitz employers had disfigured it. Faussone says to you, "Every job I undertake is like a first love." He enjoys talking about his work almost as much as he enjoys working. Faussone is Man the Worker made truly free through his labors.

Levi: I do not believe that Giulia was wrong in attributing my frenzy for work to my shyness at that time with girls. This shyness, or inhibition, was genuine, painful, and heavy—much more important for me than devotion to work. Work in the Milan factory I described in *The Periodic Table* was mock work that I did not trust. The catastrophe of the Italian armistice of September 8, 1943, was already in the air, and it would have been foolish to ignore it by digging oneself into a scientifically meaningless activity.

I have never seriously tried to analyze this shyness of mine, but no doubt Mussolini's racial laws played an important role. Other Jewish friends suffered from it, some "Aryan" schoolmates jeered at us, saying that circumcision was nothing but castration, and we, at least at an unconscious level, tended to believe it, with the help of our puritanical families. I think that *at that time* work was for me a sexual compensation rather than a real passion.

However, I am fully aware that after the camp my work, or rather my two kinds of work (chemistry and writing), did play, and still play, an essential role in my life. I am persuaded that normal human beings are biologically built for an activity that is aimed toward a goal and that idleness, or aimless work (like Auschwitz's *Arbeit*), gives rise to suffering and to atrophy. In my case, and in the case of my alter ego, Faussone, work is identical with "problem solving."

At Auschwitz I quite often observed a curious phenomenon. The need for *lavoro ben fatto*—"work properly done" —is so strong as to induce people to perform even slavish chores "properly." The Italian bricklayer who saved my life by bringing me food on the sly for six months hated Germans, their food, their language, their war; but when they set him to erect walls, he built them straight and solid, not out of obedience but out of professional dignity.

Roth: *Survival in Auschwitz* concludes with a chapter entitled "The Story of Ten Days," in which you describe, in diary form, how you endured from January 18 to January 27, 1945, among a small remnant of sick and dying patients in the camp's makeshift infirmary after the Nazis had fled westward with some twenty thousand "healthy" prisoners. What's recounted there reads to me like the story of Robinson Crusoe in hell, with you, Primo Levi, as Crusoe, wrenching what you need to live from the chaotic residue of a ruthlessly evil island. What struck me there, as throughout the book, was the extent to which thinking contributed to your survival, the thinking of a practical, humane scientific mind. Yours doesn't seem to me a survival that was determined by either brute biological strength or incredible luck. It was rooted in your professional character: the man of precision, the controller of experiments who seeks the principle of order, confronted with the evil inversion of everything he values. Granted you were a numbered part in an infernal machine, but a numbered part with a systematic mind that has always to understand. At Auschwitz you tell yourself, "I think too much" to resist, "I am too civilized." But to me the civilized man who thinks too much is

7

inseparable from the survivor. The scientist and the survivor are one.

Levi: Exactly—you hit the bull's eye. In those memorable ten days, I truly did feel like Robinson Crusoe, but with one important difference. Crusoe set to work for his individual survival, whereas I and my two French companions were consciously and happily willing to work at last for a just and human goal, to save the lives of our sick comrades.

As for survival, this is a question that I put to myself many times and that many have put to me. I insist there was no general rule, except entering the camp in good health and knowing German. Barring this, luck dominated. I have seen the survival of shrewd people and silly people, the brave and the cowardly, "thinkers" and madmen. In my case, luck played an essential role on at least two occasions: in leading me to meet the Italian bricklayer and in my getting sick only once, but at the right moment.

And yet what you say, that for me thinking and observing were survival factors, is true, although in my opinion sheer luck prevailed. I remember having lived my Auschwitz year in a condition of exceptional spiritedness. I don't know if this depended on my professional background, or an unsuspected stamina, or on a sound instinct. I never stopped recording the world and people around me, so much that I still have an unbelievably detailed image of them. I had an intense wish to understand, I was constantly pervaded by a curiosity that somebody afterward did, in fact, deem nothing less than cynical: the curiosity of the naturalist who finds himself transplanted into an environment that is monstrous but new, monstrously new.

I agree with your observation that my phrase "I think too much . . . I am too civilized" is inconsistent with this other frame of mind. Please grant me the right to inconsistency: in the camp our state of mind was unstable, it oscillated from hour to hour between hope and despair. The coherence I think one notes in my books is an artifact, a rationalization a posteriori.

Roth: *Survival in Auschwitz* was originally published in English as *If This Is a Man,* a faithful rendering of your Italian title, *Se questo è un uomo* (and the title that your first American publishers should have had the good sense to preserve). The description and analysis of your atrocious memories of the Germans' "gigantic biological and social experiment" are governed precisely by a quantitative concern for the ways in which a man can be transformed or broken down and, like a substance decomposing in a chemical reaction, lose his characteristic properties. *If This Is a Man* reads like the memoir of a theoretician of moral biochemistry who has himself been forcibly enlisted as the specimen organism to undergo laboratory experimentation of the most sinister kind. The creature caught in the laboratory of the mad scientist is himself the epitome of the rational scientist.

In *The Monkey's Wrench,* which might accurately have been titled *This Is a Man,* you tell Faussone, your blue-collar Scheherazade, that "being a chemist in the world's eyes, and feeling . . . a writer's blood in my veins" you consequently have "two souls in my body, and that's too many." I'd say there's one soul, enviably capacious and seamless; I'd say that not only are the survivor and the scientist inseparable but so are the writer and the scientist.

Levi: Rather than a question, this is a diagnosis, which I accept with thanks. I lived my camp life as rationally as I could, and I wrote *If This Is a Man* struggling to explain to others, and to myself, the events I had been involved in, but with no definite literary intention. My model (or, if you prefer, my style) was that of the "weekly report" commonly used in factories: it must be precise, concise, and written in a language comprehensible to everybody in the industrial hierarchy. And certainly not written in scientific jargon. By the way, I am not a scientist, nor have I ever been. I did want to become one, but war and the camp prevented me. I had to limit myself to being a technician throughout my professional life.

I agree with you about there being only "one soul . . . and seamless," and once more I feel grateful to you. My statement that "two souls . . . is too many" is half a joke but half hints at serious things. I worked in a factory for almost thirty years, and I must admit that there is no incompatibility between being a chemist and being a writer—in fact, there is a mutual reinforcement. But factory life, and particularly factory managing, involves many other matters, far from chemistry: hiring and firing workers; quarreling with the boss, customers, and suppliers; coping with accidents; being called to the telephone, even at night or when at a party; dealing with bureaucracy; and many more soul-destroying tasks. This whole trade is brutally incompatible with writing, which requires a fair amount of peace of mind. Consequently I felt hugely relieved when I reached retirement age and could resign, and so renounce my soul number one.

Roth: Your sequel to *If This Is a Man* (*The Reawakening*, also unfortunately retitled by one of your early American publishers) was called in Italian *La tregua*, "the truce." It's about your journey from Auschwitz back to Italy. There is a legendary dimension to that tortuous journey, especially to the story of your long gestation period in the Soviet Union, waiting to be repatriated. What's surprising about *The Truce,* which might understandably have been marked by a mood of mourning and inconsolable despair, is its exuberance. Your reconciliation with life takes place in a world that sometimes seemed to you like the primeval Chaos. Yet you are engaged by everyone, so highly entertained as well as instructed that I wonder if, despite the hunger and the cold and the fears, even despite the memories, you've ever really had a better time than during those months you call "a parenthesis of unlimited availability, a providential but unrepeatable gift of fate."

You appear to be someone who requires, above all, rootedness—in his profession, his ancestry, his region, his language—and yet when you found yourself as alone and uprooted as a man can be, you considered that condition a gift.

Levi: A friend of mine, an excellent doctor, told me many years ago: "Your remembrances of before and after are in black and white; those of Auschwitz and of your travel home are in Technicolor." He was right. Family, home, factory are good things in themselves, but they deprived me of something that I still miss: adventure. Destiny decided that I should find adventure in the awful mess of a Europe swept by war.

You are in the business, so you know how these things happen. *The Truce* was written fourteen years after *If This Is a Man;* it is a more "self-conscious" book, more methodical, more literary, the language much more profoundly elaborated. It tells the truth, but filtered truth. It was preceded by countless verbal versions. I mean, I had recounted each adventure many times, to people at widely different cultural levels (to friends mainly, and to high school boys and girls), and I had retouched it en route so as to arouse their most favorable reactions. When *If This Is a Man* began to achieve some success, and I began to see a future for my writing, I set out to put these adventures on paper. I aimed at having fun in writing and at amusing my prospective readers. Consequently I gave emphasis to strange, exotic, cheerful episodes—mainly to the Russians seen close up—and I relegated to the first and last pages the mood, as you put it, "of mourning and inconsolable despair."

I must remind you that the book was written around 1961; these were the years of Khrushchev, of Kennedy, of Pope John, of the first thaw and of great hopes. In Italy, for the first time, you could speak of the USSR in objective terms without being called a philo-Communist by the right wing and a disruptive reactionary by the powerful Italian Communist Party.

As for "rootedness," it is true that I have deep roots and that I had the luck of not losing them. My family was almost completely spared by the Nazi slaughter. The desk here where I write occupies, according to family legend, exactly the spot where I first saw light. When I found myself as "uprooted as a man can be," certainly I suffered, but this was far more than compensated for afterward by the fascination of adventure, by human encounters, by the sweetness of "convalescence" from the plague of Auschwitz. In its historical reality, my Russian "truce" turned to a "gift" only many years later, when I purified it by rethinking it and by writing about it.

Roth: You begin *The Periodic Table* by speaking of your Jewish ancestors, who arrived in Piedmont from Spain, by way of Provence, in 1500. You describe your family roots in

Piedmont and Turin as "not enormous, but deep, extensive, and fantastically intertwined." You supply a brief lexicon of the jargon these Jews concocted and used primarily as a secret language from the Gentiles, an argot composed of words derived from Hebrew roots but with Piedmontese endings. To an outsider your rootedness in this Jewish world of your forebears seems not only intertwined but, in an essential way, identical with your rootedness in the region. However, in 1938, when the racial laws were introduced restricting the freedom of Italian Jews, you came to consider being Jewish an "impurity," though, as you say in *The Periodic Table*, "I began to be proud of being impure."

The tension between your rootedness and your impurity makes me think of something that Professor Arnaldo Momigliano wrote about the Jews of Italy, that "the Jews were less a part of Italian life than they thought they were." How much a part of Italian life do you think *you* are? Do you remain an impurity, "a grain of salt or mustard," or has that sense of distinctness disappeared?

Levi: I see no contradiction between "rootedness" and being (or feeling) "a grain of mustard." To feel oneself a catalyst, a spur to one's cultural environment, a something or a somebody that confers taste and sense to life, you don't need racial laws or anti-Semitism or racism in general; however, it is an advantage to belong to a (not necessarily racial) minority. In other words, it can prove useful not to be pure. If I may return to the question: don't you feel yourself, you, Philip Roth, "rooted" in your country and at the same time "a mustard grain"? In your books I perceive a sharp mustard flavor.

I think this is the meaning of your quotation from Arnaldo Momigliano. Italian Jews (but the same can be said of the Jews of many other nations) made an important contribution to their country's cultural and political life without renouncing their identity, in fact by keeping faith with their cultural tradition. To possess two traditions, as happens to Jews but not only to Jews, is a richness—for writers but not only for writers.

I feel slightly uneasy replying to your explicit question. Yes, sure, I am a part of Italian life. Several of my books are read and discussed in high schools. I receive lots of letters—intelligent, silly, senseless—of appreciation, less frequently dissenting and quarrelsome. I receive useless manuscripts by would-be writers. My "distinctness" has changed in nature: I don't feel an *emarginato,* ghettoized, an outlaw, anymore, as in Italy there is actually no anti-Semitism. In fact, Judaism is viewed with interest and mostly with sympathy, although with mixed feelings toward Israel.

In my own way I have remained an impurity, an anomaly, but now for reasons other than before: not especially as a Jew but as an Auschwitz survivor and as an outsider-writer, coming not from the literary or university establishment but from the industrial world.

Roth: *If Not Now, When?* is like nothing else of yours that I've read in English. Though pointedly drawn from actual historical events, the book is cast as a straightforward picaresque adventure tale about a small band of Jewish partisans of Russian and Polish extraction harassing the Germans behind their Eastern frontlines. Your other books are perhaps less "imaginary" as to subject matter but strike me as more imaginative in technique. The motive behind *If Not Now, When?* seems more narrowly tendentious—and consequently less liberating to the writer—than the impulse that generates the autobiographical works.

I wonder if you agree with this: if in writing about the bravery of the Jews who fought back, you felt yourself doing something you *ought* to do, responsible to moral and political claims that don't necessarily intervene elsewhere, even when the subject is your own markedly Jewish fate.

Levi: *If Not Now, When?* is a book that followed an unforeseen path. The motivations that drove me to write it are manifold. Here they are, in order of importance.

I had made a sort of bet with myself: After so much plain or disguised autobiography, are you or are you not a fully fledged writer, capable of constructing a novel, shaping character, describing landscapes you have never seen? Try it!

I intended to amuse myself by writing a "Western" plot set in a landscape uncommon in Italy. I intended to amuse my readers by telling them a substantially optimistic story, a story of hope, even occasionally cheerful, although projected onto a background of massacre.

I wished to assault a commonplace still prevailing in Italy: a Jew is a mild person, a scholar (religious or profane), unwarlike, humiliated, who tolerated centuries of persecution without ever fighting back. It seemed to me a duty to pay homage to those Jews who, in desperate conditions, found the courage and the skill to resist.

I cherished the ambition to be the first (perhaps the only) Italian writer to describe the Yiddish world. I intended to "exploit" my popularity in my country in order to impose upon my readers a book centered on the Ashkenazi civilization, history, language, and frame of mind, all of which are virtually unknown in Italy, except by some sophisticated readers of Joseph Roth, Bellow, Singer, Malamud, Potok, and of course you.

Personally, I am satisfied with this book, mainly because

I had good fun planning and writing it. For the first and only time in my life as a writer, I had the impression (almost a hallucination) that my characters were alive, around me, behind my back, suggesting spontaneously their feats and their dialogues. The year I spent writing was a happy one, and so, whatever the result, for me this was a liberating book.

Roth: Let's talk about the paint factory. In our time many writers have worked as teachers, some as journalists, and most writers over fifty, in the East or the West, have been employed, for a while at least, as somebody or other's soldier. There is an impressive list of writers who have simultaneously practiced medicine and written books and of others who have been clergymen. T. S. Eliot was a publisher, and as everyone knows Wallace Stevens and Franz Kafka worked for large insurance companies. To my knowledge, only two writers of importance have been managers of paint factories: you in Turin, Italy, and Sherwood Anderson in Elyria, Ohio. Anderson had to leave the paint factory (and his family) to become a writer; you seem to have become the writer you are by staying and pursuing your career there. I wonder if you think of yourself as actually more fortunate—even better equipped to write—than those of us who are without a paint factory and all that's implied by that kind of connection.

Levi: As I have already said, I entered the paint industry by chance, but I never had very much to do with the general run of paints, varnishes, and lacquers. Our company, immediately after it began, specialized in the production of wire enamels, insulating coatings for copper electrical conductors. At the peak of my career, I numbered among the thirty or forty specialists in the world in this branch. The animals hanging here on the wall are made out of scrap enameled wire.

Honestly, I knew nothing of Sherwood Anderson till you spoke of him. No, it would never have occurred to me to quit family and factory for full-time writing, as he did. I'd have feared the jump into the dark, and I would have lost any right to a retirement allowance.

However, to your list of writer–paint manufacturers I must add a third name, Italo Svevo, a converted Jew of Trieste, the author of *The Confessions of Zeno,* who lived from 1861 to 1928. For a long time Svevo was the commercial manager of a paint company in Trieste, the Società Venziani, that belonged to his father-in-law and that dissolved a few years ago. Until 1918 Trieste belonged to Austria, and this company was famous because it supplied the Austrian navy with an excellent antifouling paint, preventing shellfish incrustation, for the keels of warships. After 1918 Trieste became Italian, and the paint was delivered to the Italian and British navies. To be able to deal with the Admiralty, Svevo took lessons in English from James Joyce, at the time a teacher in Trieste. They became friends and Joyce assisted Svevo in finding a publisher for his works. The trade name of the antifouling paint was Moravia. That it is the same as the nom de plume of the novelist is not fortuitous: both the Trieste entrepreneur and the Roman writer derived it from the family name of a mutual relative on the mother's side. Forgive me this hardly pertinent gossip.

No, as I've hinted already, I have no regrets. I don't believe I have wasted my time in managing a factory. My factory *militanza*—my compulsory and honorable service there—kept me in touch with the world of real things.

Aharon Appelfeld

[1988]

AHARON APPELFELD lives a few miles west of Jerusalem in a mazelike conglomeration of attractive stone dwellings next to an "absorption center," where immigrants are temporarily housed, schooled, and prepared for life in their new society. The arduous journey that landed Appelfeld on the beaches of Tel Aviv in 1946, at the age of fourteen, seems to have fostered an unappeasable fascination with all uprooted souls, and at the local grocery where he and the absorption center's residents do their shopping, he will often initiate an impromptu conversation with an Ethiopian, or a Russian, or a Rumanian Jew still dressed for the climate of a country to which he or she will never return.

The living room of the two-story apartment is simply furnished: some comfortable chairs, books in three languages on the shelves, and on the walls impressive adolescent drawings by the Appelfelds' son Meir, who is now twenty-one and, since finishing his military duty, has been studying art in London. Yitzak, eighteen, recently completed high school and is in the first of his three years of compulsory army service. Still at home is twelve-year-old Batya, a clever girl with the dark hair and blue eyes of her Argentinean Jewish mother, Appelfeld's youthful, good-natured wife, Judith. The Appelfelds appear to have created as calm and harmonious a household as any child could hope to grow up in. During the four years that Aharon and I have been friends, I don't think I've ever visited him at home in Mevasseret Zion without remembering that his own childhood—as an escapee from a Nazi work camp, on his own in the primitive wilds of the Ukraine—provides the grimmest possible antithesis to this domestic ideal.

A portrait photograph that I've seen of Aharon Appelfeld, an antique-looking picture taken in Chernovtsy, Bukovina, in 1938, when Aharon was six—a picture brought to Palestine by surviving relatives—shows a delicately refined bourgeois child seated alertly on a hobbyhorse and wearing a beautiful sailor suit. You cannot imagine this child, only twenty-four months on, confronting the exigencies of surviving for years as a hunted and parentless little boy in the woods. The keen intelligence is certainly there, but where is the robust cunning, the feral instinct, the biological tenacity it took to endure that terrifying adventure?

As much is secreted away in that child as in the writer he's become. At fifty-five, Aharon is a small, bespectacled, compact man with a perfectly round face and a perfectly bald head and the playfully thoughtful air of a benign wizard. He'd have no trouble passing for a magician who entertains children at birthday parties by pulling doves out of a hat—it's easier to associate his gently affable and kindly appearance with that job than with the responsibility by which he seems inescapably propelled: responding, in a string of elusively portentous stories, to the disappearance from Europe—while he was outwitting peasants and foraging in the forests—of just about all the continent's Jews, his parents among them.

His literary subject is not the Holocaust, however, or even Jewish persecution. Nor, to my mind, is what he writes Jewish fiction or, for that matter, Israeli fiction. Nor, since he is a Jewish citizen of a Jewish state composed largely of immigrants, is his an exile's fiction. And, despite the European locale of many of his novels and the echoes of Kafka, these books written in the Hebrew language aren't European fiction. Indeed, all that Appelfeld is not adds up to what he is, and that is a dislocated writer, a deported writer, a dispossessed and uprooted writer. Appelfeld is a displaced writer of displaced fiction, who has made of displacement and disorientation a subject uniquely his own. His sensibility—marked almost at birth by the solitary wanderings of a little bourgeois boy through an ominous nowhere—appears to have spontaneously generated a style of sparing specificity, of out-of-time progression and thwarted narrative drives, that is an uncanny prose realization of the displaced mentality. As unique as the subject is a voice that originates in a wounded consciousness pitched somewhere between amnesia and memory and that situates the fiction it narrates midway between parable and history.

Since we met in 1984, Aharon and I have talked together at great length, usually while walking through the streets of London, New York, and Jerusalem. I've known him over these years as an oracular anecdotalist and folkloristic enchanter, as a wittily laconic kibitzer and an obsessive dissector of Jewish states of mind—of Jewish aversions, delusions, remembrances, and manias. Yet as is often the case in friendships between writers, during these peripatetic conversations we had never really touched on each other's work—that is, not until last month, when I traveled to Jerusalem to discuss with him the six of his fifteen published books that are now in English translation.

After our first afternoon together we disencumbered ourselves of an interloping tape recorder and, though I took some notes along the way, mostly we talked as we've become accustomed to talking—wandering along city streets or sitting in coffee shops where we'd stop to rest. When finally there seemed to be little left to say, we sat down together and tried to synthesize on paper—I in English, Aharon in Hebrew—the heart of the discussion. Aharon's answers to my questions have been translated by Jeffrey Green.

Roth: I find echoes in your fiction of two Middle European writers of a previous generation: Bruno Schulz, the Polish Jew who wrote in Polish and was shot and killed at fifty by the Nazis in Drohobycz, the heavily Jewish Galician city where he taught high school and lived at home with his family, and Kafka, the Prague Jew who wrote in German and also lived, according to Max Brod, "spellbound in the family circle" for most of his forty-one years. You were born 500 miles east of Prague, 125 miles southeast of Drohobycz, in Chernovtsy. Your family—prosperous, highly assimilated, German-speaking—bore certain cultural and social similarities to Kafka's, and, like Schulz, you, along with your family, suffered personally the Nazi horror. The affinity that interests me, however, isn't biographical but literary, and though I see signs of it throughout your work, it's particularly clear in *The Age of Wonders*. The opening scene, for instance, depicting a mother and her adoring twelve-year-old luxuriating on a train journey home from their idyllic summer vacation, reminds me of similar scenes in Schulz stories. And only a few pages on, there is a Kafkaesque surprise when the train stops unexpectedly by a dark old sawmill and the security forces request that "all Austrian passengers who are not Christians by birth" register at the sawmill's office. I'm reminded of *The Trial*—of *The Castle* as well—where there is at the outset an ambiguously menacing assault on the legal status of the hero. Tell me, how pertinent to your imagination do you consider Kafka and Schulz to be?

Appelfeld: I discovered Kafka here in Israel during the 1950s, and as a writer he was close to me from my first contact. He spoke to me in my mother tongue, German—not the German of the Germans but the German of the Hapsburg Empire, of Vienna, Prague, and Chernovtsy, with its special tone, which, by the way, the Jews worked hard to create.

To my surprise he spoke to me not only in my mother tongue but also in another language that I knew intimately, the language of the absurd. I knew what he was talking about. It wasn't a secret language for me and I didn't need any explications. I had come from the camps and the forests, from a world that embodied the absurd, and nothing in that world was foreign to me. What was surprising was this: how could a man who had never been there know so much, in precise detail, about that world?

Other surprising discoveries followed: the marvel of his objective style, his preference for action over interpretation, his clarity and precision, the broad, comprehensive view laden with humor and irony. And, as if that weren't enough, another discovery showed me that behind the mask of placelessness and homelessness in his work stood a Jewish man, like me, from a half-assimilated family, whose Jewish values had lost their content and whose inner space was barren and haunted.

The marvelous thing is that the barrenness brought him not to self-denial or self-hatred but rather to a kind of tense curiosity about every Jewish phenomenon, especially the Jews of Eastern Europe, the Yiddish language, the Yiddish theater, Hasidism, Zionism, and even the ideal of moving to Mandate Palestine. This is the Kafka of his journals, which are no less gripping than his works. I found a palpable embodiment of Kafka's Jewish involvement in his Hebrew handwriting, for he had studied Hebrew and knew it. His handwriting is clear and amazingly beautiful, showing his effort and concentration as in his German handwriting, but his Hebrew handwriting has an additional aura of love for the isolated letter.

Kafka revealed to me not only the plan of the absurd world but also the charms of its art, which I needed as an assimilated Jew. The fifties were years of search for me, and Kafka's works illuminated the narrow path that I tried to blaze for myself. Kafka emerges from an inner world and tries to get some grip on reality, and I came from a world of detailed, empirical reality, the camps and the forests. My real world was far beyond the power of imagination, and my task as an artist was not to develop my imagination but to restrain it, and even then it seemed impossible to me, because everything was so unbelievable that one seemed oneself to be fictional.

At first I tried to run away from myself and from my memories, to live a life that was not my own and to write about a life that was not my own. But a hidden feeling told me that I was not allowed to flee from myself and that if I denied the experience of my childhood in the Holocaust, I would be spiritually deformed. Only when I reached the age of thirty did I feel the freedom to deal as an artist with those experiences.

To my regret, I came to Bruno Schulz's work years too late, after my literary approach was rather well formed. I felt and still feel a great affinity with his writing, but not the same affinity I feel with Kafka.

Roth: Of your six books translated now into English, *The Age of Wonders* is the one in which an identifiable historical background is most sharply delineated. The narrator's writer-father is an admirer of Kafka's; in addition, the father is party, we are told, to an intellectual debate about Martin Buber; we're also told that he's a friend of Stefan Zweig's. But this specificity, even if it doesn't develop much beyond these few references to an outside world, is not common in the books of yours I've read. Hardship generally fells your Jews the way the overpowering ordeal descends on Kafka's victims: inexplicably, out of nowhere, in a society seemingly without history or politics. "What do they want of us?" asks a Jew in *Badenheim 1939*, after he's gone to register as a Jew at, of all places, the Badenheim Sanitation Department. "It's hard to understand," another Jew answers.

There's no news from the public realm that might serve as a warning to an Appelfeld victim, nor is the victim's impending doom presented as part of a European catastrophe. The historical focus is supplied by the reader, who understands, as the victims cannot, the magnitude of the enveloping evil. Your reticence as a historian, when combined with the historical perspective of a knowing reader, accounts for the peculiar impact your work has, for the power that emanates from stories that are told through such modest means. Also, dehistoricizing the events and blurring the background, you probably approximate the disorientation felt by people who were unaware that they were on the brink of a cataclysm.

It's occurred to me that the perspective of the adults in your fiction resembles in its limitations the viewpoint of a child, who has no historical calendar in which to place unfolding events and no intellectual means of penetrating their meaning. I wonder if your own consciousness as a child at the edge of the Holocaust isn't mirrored in the simplicity with which the imminent horror is perceived in your novels.

Appelfeld: You're right. In *Badenheim 1939* I completely ignored the historical explanation. I assumed that the historical facts were known to readers and that they would fill in what was missing. You're also correct, it seems to me, in assuming that my description of the Second World War has something in it of a child's vision, but I'm not sure whether the ahistorical quality of *Badenheim 1939* derives from the child's vision that's preserved within me. Historical explanations have been alien to me ever since I became aware of myself as an artist. And the Jewish experience in the Second World War was not "historical." We came into contact with archaic mythical forces, a kind of dark subconscious the meaning of which we did not know, nor do we know it to this day. This world appears to be rational (with trains, departure times, stations, and engineers), but in fact these were journeys of the imagination, lies and ruses, which only deep, irrational drives could have invented. I didn't understand, nor do I yet understand, the motives of the murderers.

I was a victim, and I try to understand the victim. That is

a broad, complicated expanse of life that I've been trying to deal with for thirty years now. I haven't idealized the victims. I don't think that in *Badenheim 1939* there's any idealization either. By the way, Badenheim is a rather real place, and spas like that were scattered all over Europe, shockingly petit bourgeois and idiotic in their formalities. Even as a child I saw how ridiculous they were.

It is generally agreed, to this day, that Jews are deft, cunning, and sophisticated creatures, with the wisdom of the world stored up in them. But isn't it fascinating to see how easy it was to fool the Jews? With the simplest, almost childish tricks they were gathered up in ghettos, starved for months, encouraged with false hopes, and finally sent to their deaths by train. That ingenuousness stood before my eyes while I was writing *Badenheim*. In that ingenuousness I found a kind of distillation of humanity. Their blindness and deafness, their obsessive preoccupation with themselves, is an integral part of their ingenuousness. The murderers were practical, and they knew just what they wanted. The ingenuous person is always a shlemazl, a clownish victim of misfortune, never hearing the danger signals in time, getting mixed up, tangled up, and finally falling in the trap. Those weaknesses charmed me. I fell in love with them. The myth that the Jews run the world with their machinations turned out to be somewhat exaggerated.

Roth: Of all your translated books, *Tzili* depicts the harshest reality and the most extreme suffering. Tzili, the simple child of a poor Jewish family, is left alone when her family flees the Nazi invasion. The novel recounts her horrendous adventures in surviving and her excruciating loneliness among the brutal peasants for whom she works. The book strikes me as a counterpart to Jerzy Kosinski's *Painted Bird*.

Though less grotesque, *Tzili* portrays a fearful child in a world even bleaker and more barren than Kosinski's, a child moving in isolation through a landscape as uncongenial to human life as any in Beckett's *Molloy*.

As a boy you wandered alone like Tzili after your escape, at eight, from the camp. I've been wondering why, when you came to transform your own life in an unknown place, hiding out among the hostile peasants, you decided to imagine a girl as the survivor of this ordeal. And did it occur to you ever *not* to fictionalize this material but to present your experiences as you remember them, to write a survivor's tale as direct, say, as Primo Levi's depiction of his Auschwitz incarceration?

Appelfeld: I have never written about things as they happened. All my works are indeed chapters from my most personal experience, but nevertheless they are not "the story of my life." The things that happened to me in my life have already happened, they are already formed, and time has kneaded them and given them shape. To write things as they happened means to enslave oneself to memory, which is only a minor element in the creative process. To my mind, to create means to order, sort out, and choose the words and the pace that fit the work. The materials are indeed materials from one's life, but ultimately the creation is an independent creature.

I tried several times to write "the story of my life" in the woods after I ran away from the camp. But all my efforts were in vain. I wanted to be faithful to reality and to what really happened. But the chronicle that emerged proved to be a weak scaffolding. The result was rather meager, an unconvincing imaginary tale. The things that are most true are easily falsified.

Reality, as you know, is always stronger than the human imagination. Not only that, reality can permit itself to be unbelievable, inexplicable, out of all proportion. The created work, to my regret, cannot permit itself all that.

The reality of the Holocaust surpassed any imagination. If I remained true to the fact, no one would believe me. But the moment I chose a girl, a little older than I was at that time, I removed "the story of my life" from the mighty grip of memory and gave it over to the creative laboratory. There memory is not the only proprietor. There one needs a causal explanation, a thread to tie things together. The exceptional is permissible only if it is part of an overall structure and contributes to its understanding. I had to remove those parts that were unbelievable from "the story of my life" and present a more credible version.

When I wrote *Tzili* I was about forty years old. At that time I was interested in the possibilities of naiveness in art. Can there be a naive modern art? It seemed to me that without the naiveté still found among children and old people and, to some extent, in ourselves, the work of art would be flawed. I tried to correct that flaw. God knows how successful I was.

Roth: *Badenheim 1939* has been called fablelike, dreamlike, nightmarish, and so on. None of these descriptions makes the book less vexing to me. The reader is asked—pointedly, I think—to understand the transformation of a pleasant Austrian resort for Jews into a grim staging area for Jewish "relocation" to Poland as being somehow analogous to events preceding Hitler's Holocaust. At the same time your vision of Badenheim and its Jewish inhabitants is almost impulsively antic and indifferent to matters of causality. It isn't that a menacing situation develops, as it frequently does in life, without warning or logic, but that about these events you are laconic, I think, to the point of unrewarding inscrutability. Do you mind addressing my difficulties as a reader with this highly praised novel, which is perhaps your most famous book in America? What is the relation between the fictional world of *Badenheim* and historical reality?

Appelfeld: Rather clear childhood memories underlie *Badenheim 1939*. Every summer we, like all the other petit-bourgeois families, would set out for a resort. Every summer we tried to find a restful place where people didn't gossip in the corridors, didn't confess to one another in corners, didn't interfere with you, and, of course, didn't speak Yiddish. But every summer, as though we were being spited, we were once again surrounded by Jews, and that left a bad taste in my parents' mouths, and no small amount of anger.

Many years after the Holocaust, when I came to retrace my childhood from before the Holocaust, I saw that these resorts occupied a particular place in my memories. Many faces and bodily twitches came back to life. It turned out that the grotesque was etched in, no less than the tragic. Walks in the woods and the elaborate meals brought people together in Badenheim—to speak to one another and to confess to one another. People permitted themselves not only to dress extravagantly but also to speak freely, sometimes picturesquely. Husbands occasionally lost their lovely wives, and from time to time a shot would ring out in the evening, a sharp sign of disappointed love. Of course I could arrange these precious scraps of life to stand on their own artistically. But what was I to do? Every time I tried to reconstruct those forgotten resorts, I had visions of the trains and the camps, and my most hidden childhood memories were spotted with the soot from the trains.

Fate was already hidden within those people like a mortal illness. Assimilated Jews built a structure of humanistic values and looked out on the world from it. They were certain that they were no longer Jews and that what applied to "the Jews" did not apply to them. That strange assurance made them into blind or half-blind creatures. I have always loved assimilated Jews, because that was where the Jewish character, and also perhaps Jewish fate, was concentrated with the greatest force.

In *Badenheim* I tried to combine sights from my childhood with sights of the Holocaust. My feeling was that I had to remain faithful to both realms. That is, that I must not prettify the victims but rather depict them in full light, unadorned, but at the same time that I had to point out the fate hidden within them, though they do not know it.

That is a very narrow bridge, without a railing, and it's very easy to fall off.

Roth: Not until you reached Palestine, in 1946, did you come in contact with Hebrew. What effect do you think this had on your Hebrew prose? Are you aware of any special connection between how you came to Hebrew and how you write in Hebrew?

Appelfeld: My mother tongue was German. My grandparents spoke Yiddish. Most of the inhabitants of Bukovina, where I lived as a child, were Ruthenians and so they all spoke Ruthenian. The government was Rumanian, and everyone was required to speak that language as well. When the Second World War broke out, and I was eight, I was deported to a camp in Transmistria. After I ran away from the camp I lived among the Ukrainians, and so I learned Ukrainian. In 1944 I was liberated by the Russian army and I worked for them as a messenger boy, and that's how I came by my knowledge of Russian. For two years, from 1944 to 1946, I wandered all over Europe and picked up other languages. When I finally reached Palestine in 1946, my head was full of tongues, but the truth of the matter is that I had no language.

I learned Hebrew by dint of much effort. It is a difficult language, severe and ascetic. Its ancient basis is the proverb from the Mishna: "Silence is a fence for wisdom." The Hebrew language taught me how to think, to be sparing with words, not to use too many adjectives, not to intervene too much, and not to interpret. I say that it "taught me." In fact, those are the demands it makes. If it weren't for Hebrew, I doubt whether I would have found my way to Judaism. Hebrew offered me the heart of the Jewish myth, its way of thinking and its beliefs, from the days of the Bible to Agnon. This is a thick strand of five thousand years of Jewish creativity, with all its rises and falls: the poetic language of the Bible, the juridical language of the Talmud, and the mystical language of the Kabala. This richness is sometimes difficult to cope with. Sometimes one is stifled by too many associations, by the multitude of worlds hidden in the single word. But never mind, those are marvelous resources. Ultimately you find in them even more than you were looking for.

Like most of the other kids who came to this country as Holocaust survivors, I wanted to run away from my memories, from my Jewishness, and to build up a different image for myself. What didn't we do to change, to be tall, blond, and strong, to be goyim, with all the outer trappings. The Hebrew language also sounded like a Gentile language to us, which is perhaps why we fell in love with it so easily.

But then something amazing happened. That very language, which we saw as a means of melting into self-forgetfulness and merging with the Israeli celebration of the land and heroism, that language tricked me and brought me, against my will, to the most secret storehouses of Judaism. Since then I haven't budged from there.

Roth: Living in this society you are bombarded by news and political disputation. Yet, as a novelist, you have by and large pushed aside the Israeli daily turbulence to contemplate markedly different Jewish predicaments. What does this turbulence mean to a novelist like yourself? How does being a citizen of this self-revealing, self-asserting, self-challenging, self-legendizing society affect your writing life? Does the news-producing reality ever tempt your imagination?

Appelfeld: Your question touches on a matter that is very important to me. True, Israel is full of drama from morning to night, and there are people who are overcome by that drama to the point of inebriation. This frenetic activity isn't only the result of pressure from the outside. Jewish restlessness contributes its part. Everything is buzzing here, and dense. There's a lot of talk, the controversies rage. The Jewish shtetl has not disappeared.

At one time there was a strong anti-Diaspora tendency here, a recoiling from anything Jewish. Today things have changed a bit, though this country is restless and tangled up in itself, living with ups and downs. Today we have redemption, tomorrow darkness. Writers are also immersed in this tangle. The occupied territories, for example, are not only a political issue but also a literary matter.

I came here in 1946, still a boy but burdened with life

and suffering. In the daytime I worked on kibbutz farms and at night I studied Hebrew. For many years I wandered about this feverish country, lost and lacking any orientation. I was looking for myself and for the face of my parents, who had been lost in the Holocaust. During the 1940s one had a feeling that one was being reborn here as a Jew, and one would therefore turn out to be quite a wonder. Every utopian view produces that kind of atmosphere. Let's not forget that this was after the Holocaust. To be strong was not merely a matter of ideology. "Never again like sheep to the slaughter" thundered from loudspeakers at every corner. I very much wished to fit into that great activity and take part in the adventure of the birth of a new nation. Naively I believed that action would silence my memories and I would flourish like the natives, free of the Jewish nightmare, but what could I do? The need, you might say the necessity, to be faithful to myself and to my childhood memories made me a distant, contemplative person. My contemplation brought me back to the region where I was born and where my parents' home stood. That is my spiritual history, and it is from there that I spin the threads.

Artistically speaking, settling back there has given me an anchorage and a perspective. I'm not obligated to rush out to meet current events and interpret them immediately. Daily events do indeed knock on every door, but they know that I don't let such agitated guests into my house.

Roth: In *To the Land of the Cattails,* a Jewish woman and her grown son, the offspring of a Gentile father, are journeying back to the remote Ruthenian countryside where she was born. It's the summer of 1938. The closer they get to her home, the more menacing is the threat of Gentile violence. The mother says to her son: "They are many, and we are few." Then you write: "The word *goy* rose up from within her. She smiled as if hearing a distant memory. Her father would sometimes, though only occasionally, use that word to indicate hopeless obtuseness."

The Gentile with whom the Jews of your books seem to share their world is usually the embodiment of hopeless obtuseness and of menacing, primitive social behavior— the goy as drunkard, wife beater, as the coarse, brutal semi-savage who is "not in control of himself." Though obviously there's more to be said about the non-Jewish world in those provinces where your books are set—and about the capacity of Jews, in their own world, also to be obtuse and primitive—even a non-Jewish European would have to recognize that the power of this image over the Jewish imagination is rooted in real experience. Alternatively the goy is pictured as an "earthy soul . . . overflowing with health." *Enviable* health. As the mother in *Cattails* says of her half-Gentile son, "He's not nervous like me. Other, quiet blood flows in his veins."

I'd say that it's impossible to know anything about the Jewish imagination without investigating the place that the goy has occupied in the folk mythology that's been exploited, in America, at one level by comedians like Lenny Bruce and Jackie Mason and, at quite another level, by Jewish novelists. American fiction's most single-minded portrait of the goy is in *The Assistant* by Bernard Malamud. The goy is Frank Alpine, the down-and-out thief who robs the failing grocery store of the Jew, Bober, later attempts to rape Bober's studious daughter, and eventually, in a conversion to Bober's brand of suffering Judaism, symbolically renounces goyish savagery. The New York Jewish hero of Saul Bellow's second novel, *The Victim,* is plagued by an alcoholic Gentile misfit named Allbee, who is no less of a bum and a drifter than Alpine, even if his assault on Leventhal's hard-won composure is intellectually more urbane. The most imposing Gentile in all of Bellow's work, however, is Henderson—the self-exploring rain king who, to restore his psychic health, takes his blunted instincts off to Africa. For Bellow no less than for Appelfeld, the truly "earthy soul" is not the Jew, nor is the search to retrieve primitive energies portrayed as the quest of a Jew. For Bellow no less than for Appelfeld, and, astonishingly, for Mailer no less than for Appelfeld—we all know that in Mailer when a man is a sadistic sexual aggressor his name is Sergius O'Shaugnessy, when he is a wife killer his name is Stephen Rojack, and when he is a menacing murderer he isn't Lepke Buchalter or Gurrah Shapiro, he's Gary Gilmore.

Appelfeld: The place of the non-Jew in the Jewish imagination is a complex affair growing out of generations of Jewish fear. Which of us dares to take up the burden of explanation? I will hazard only a few words, something from my personal experience.

I said fear, but the fear wasn't uniform, and it wasn't of all Gentiles. In fact, there was a sort of envy of the non-Jew hidden in the heart of the modern Jew. The non-Jew was frequently viewed in the Jewish imagination as a liberated creature without ancient beliefs or social obligation who lived a natural life on his own soil. The Holocaust, of course, altered somewhat the course of the Jewish imagination. In place of envy came suspicion. The feelings that had walked in the open descended to the underground.

Is there some stereotype of the non-Jew in the Jewish soul? It exists, and it is frequently embodied in the word *goy*, but that is an undeveloped stereotype. The Jews have had imposed on them too many moral and religious strictures to express such feelings utterly without restraint. Among the Jews there was never the confidence to express verbally the depths of hostility they may well have felt. They were, for good or bad, too rational. What hostility they permitted themselves to feel was, paradoxically, directed at themselves.

What has preoccupied me, and continues to perturb me, is this anti-Semitism directed at oneself, an ancient Jewish ailment which in modern times has taken on various guises. I grew up in an assimilated Jewish home where German was treasured. German was considered not only a language but also a culture, and the attitude toward German culture was virtually religious. All around us lived masses of Jews who spoke Yiddish, but in our home Yiddish was absolutely forbidden. I grew up with the feeling that anything Jewish was blemished. From my earliest childhood my gaze was directed at the beauty of non-Jews. They were blond and tall and behaved naturally. They were cultured, and when they didn't behave in a cultured fashion, at least they behaved naturally.

Our housemaid illustrated that theory well. She was pretty and buxom, and I was attached to her. She was, in my eyes, the eyes of a child, nature itself, and when she ran off with my mother's jewelry, I saw that as no more than a forgivable mistake.

From my earliest youth I was drawn to non-Jews. They fascinated me with their strangeness, their height, their aloofness. Yet the Jews seemed strange to me too. It took years to understand how much my parents had internalized all the evil they attributed to the Jew, and, through them, I did also. A hard kernel of revulsion was planted within each of us.

The change took place in me when we were uprooted from our house and driven into the ghettos. Then I noticed that all the doors and windows of our non-Jewish neighbors were suddenly shut, and we walked alone in the empty streets. None of our many neighbors, with whom we had connections, was at the window when we dragged along our suitcases. I say "the change," and that isn't the entire truth. I was eight years old then, and the whole world seemed like a nightmare to me. Afterward too, when I was separated from my parents, I didn't know why. All during the war I wandered among the Ukrainian villages, keeping my hidden secret: my Jewishness. Fortunately for me, I was blond and didn't arouse suspicion.

It took me years to draw close to the Jew within me. I had to get rid of many prejudices within me and to meet many Jews in order to find myself in them. Anti-Semitism directed at oneself was an original Jewish creation. I don't know of any other nation so flooded with self-criticism. Even after the Holocaust, Jews did not seem blameless in their own eyes. On the contrary, harsh comments were made by prominent Jews against the victims, for not protecting themselves and fighting back. The ability of Jews to internalize any critical and condemnatory remark and castigate themselves is one of the marvels of human nature.

The feeling of guilt has settled and taken refuge among all the Jews who want to reform the world, the various kinds of socialists, anarchists, but mainly among Jewish artists. Day and night the flame of that feeling produces dread, sensitivity, self-criticism, and sometimes self-destruction. In short, it isn't a particularly glorious feeling. Only one thing may be said in its favor: it harms no one except those afflicted with it.

Roth: In *The Immortal Bartfuss,* Bartfuss asks "irreverently" of his dying mistress's ex-husband, "What have we Holocaust survivors done? Has our great experience changed us at all?" This is the question with which the novel somehow engages itself on virtually every page. We sense in Bartfuss's lonely longing and regret, in his baffled effort to overcome his own remoteness, in his avidity for human contact, in his mute wanderings along the Israeli coast and his enigmatic encounters in dirty cafés, the agony that life can become in the wake of a great disaster. Of the Jewish survivors who wind up smuggling and black-marketeering in Italy right after the war, you write, "No one knew what to do with the lives that had been saved."

My last question, growing out of your preoccupation in *The Immortal Bartfuss,* is perhaps preposterously comprehensive. From what you observed as a homeless youngster wandering in Europe after the war, and from what you've learned during four decades in Israel, do you discern distinguishing patterns in the experience of those whose lives were saved? What *have* the Holocaust survivors done and in what ways *were* they ineluctably changed?

Appelfeld: True, that is the painful point of my latest book. Indirectly I tried to answer your question there. Now I'll try to expand somewhat. The Holocaust belongs to the type of enormous experience that reduces one to silence. Any utterance, any statement, any "answer" is tiny, meaningless, and occasionally ridiculous. Even the greatest of answers seems petty.

With your permission, two examples. The first is Zionism. Without doubt, life in Israel gives the survivors not only a place of refuge but also a feeling that the entire world is not evil. Though the tree has been chopped down, the root has not withered—despite everything, we continue living. Yet that satisfaction cannot take away the survivor's feeling that he or she must do something with this life that was saved. The survivors have undergone experiences that no one else has undergone, and others expect some message from them, some key to understanding the human world—a human example. But they, of course, cannot begin to fulfill the great tasks imposed upon them, so theirs are clandestine lives of flight and hiding. The trouble is that no more hiding places are available. One has a feeling of guilt that grows from year to year and becomes, as in Kafka, an accusation. The wound is too deep and bandages won't help. Not even a bandage such as the Jewish state.

The second example is the religious stance. Paradoxically, as a gesture toward their murdered parents, not a few survivors have adopted religious faith. I know what inner struggles that paradoxical stance entails, and I respect it. But that stance is born of despair. I won't deny the truth of despair. But it's a suffocating position, a kind of Jewish monasticism and indirect self-punishment.

My book offers its survivor neither Zionist nor religious consolation. The survivor, Bartfuss, has swallowed the Holocaust whole, and he walks about with it in all his limbs. He drinks the "black milk" of the poet Paul Celan, morning, noon, and night. He has no advantage over anyone else, but he still hasn't lost his human face. That isn't a great deal, but it's something.

Ivan Klíma

[1990]

BORN IN PRAGUE in 1931, Ivan Klíma has undergone
what Jan Kott calls a "European education": during
his adult years as a novelist, critic, and playwright his
work was suppressed in Czechoslovakia by the Communist
authorities (and his family members harried and punished
right along with him), while during his early years, as a
Jewish child, he was transported, with his parents, to the
Terezin concentration camp by the Nazis. In 1968, when
the Russians moved into Czechoslovakia, he was out of the
country, in London, on the way to the University of Michi-
gan to see a production of one of his plays and to teach literature. When his teaching duties ended in Ann Arbor in
the spring of 1970, he returned to Czechoslovakia with his
wife and two children to become one of the "admirable
handful"—as a professor recently reinstated at Charles University described Klíma and his circle to me at lunch one
day—whose persistent opposition to the regime made their
daily lives extremely hard.

Of his fifteen or so novels and collections of stories,
those written after 1970 were published openly only abroad,

in Europe primarily; only two books—neither of them among his best—have appeared in America, where his work is virtually unknown. Coincidentally, Ivan Klíma's novel *Love and Garbage*, inspired in part by his months during the seventies as a Prague street cleaner, was published in Czechoslovakia on the very day in February 1990 that I flew there to see him. He arrived at the airport to pick me up after spending the morning in a Prague bookstore where readers who had just bought his book waited for him to sign their copies in a line that stretched from the shop into the street. (During my week in Prague, the longest lines I saw were for ice cream and for books.) The initial printing of *Love and Garbage*, his first Czech publication in twenty years, was 100,000 copies. Later in the afternoon, he learned that a second book of his, *My Merry Mornings*, a collection of stories, had been published that day as well, also in an edition of 100,000. In the three months since censorship has been abolished, a stage play of his has been produced and a TV play has been broadcast. Five more of his books are to appear this year.

Love and Garbage is the story of a well-known, banned Czech writer "hemmed in by prohibition" and at work as a street cleaner, who for a number of years finds some freedom from the claustrophobic refuge of his home—from the trusting wife who wants to make people happy and is writing a study on self-sacrifice; from the two dearly loved growing children—with a moody, spooky, demanding sculptor, a married mother herself, who comes eventually to curse him and to slander the wife he can't leave. To this woman he is erotically addicted:

There was a lot of snow that winter. She'd take her little girl to her piano lessons. I'd walk behind them, without the child being aware of me. I'd sink into the freshly fallen snow because I wasn't looking where I was going. I was watching her walking.

It is the story of a responsible man who guiltily yearns to turn his back on all the bitter injustices and to escape into a "private region of bliss." "My ceaseless escapes" is how he reproachfully describes the figure in his carpet.

At the same time, the book is a patchwork rumination on Kafka's spirit (the writer mentally works up an essay about Kafka while he's out cleaning streets); on the meaning of soot, smoke, filth, and garbage in a world that can turn even people into garbage; on death; on hope; on fathers and sons (a dark, tender leitmotif is the final illness of the writer's father); and, among other things, on the decline of Czech into "jerkish." Jerkish is the name of the language developed in the United States some years back for the communication between people and chimpanzees; it consists of 225 words, and Klíma's hero predicts that, after what has happened to his own language under the Communists, it can't be long before jerkish is spoken by all mankind. "Over breakfast," says this writer whom the state will not allow to be published, "I'd read a poem in the paper by the leading author writing in jerkish." The four banal little quatrains are quoted. "For this poem of 69 words," he says, "including the title, the author needed a mere 37 jerkish terms and no idea at all . . . Anyone strong enough to read the poem attentively will realize that for a jerkish poet even a vocabulary of 225 words is needlessly large."

Love and Garbage is a wonderful book, marred only by some distressing lapses into philosophical banality, particularly as the central story winds down, and (in the English version published by Chatto and Windus in London) by the translator's inability to imagine a pungent, credible demotic idiom appropriate to the argot of the social misfits in Klíma's street-cleaning detail. It is an inventive book that—aside from its absurdist title—is wholly unexhibitionistic. Klíma juggles a dozen motifs and undertakes the boldest transitions without hocus-pocus, as unshowily as Chekhov telling the story "Gooseberries"; he provides a nice antidote to all that magic in magic realism. The simplicity with which he creates his elaborate collage—harrowing concentration camp memories, ecological reflections, imaginary spats between the estranged lovers, and down-to-earth Kafkean analysis, all juxtaposed and glued to the ordeal of the exhilarating, exhausting adultery—is continuous with the disarming directness, verging on adolescent ingenuousness, with which the patently autobiographical hero confesses his emotional turmoil.

The book is permeated by an intelligence whose tenderness colors everything and is unchecked and unguarded by irony. Klíma is, in this regard, Milan Kundera's antithesis— an observation that might seem superfluous were it not for the correspondence of preoccupations. The temperamental divide between the two is considerable, their origins diverge as sharply as the paths they've taken as men, and yet their affinity for the erotically vulnerable, their struggle against political despair, their brooding over social excreta, whether garbage or kitsch, a shared inclination for extended commentary and for mixing modes—not to mention their fixation on the fate of outcasts—create an odd, tense kinship, one not as unlikely as it might seem to both writers. I sometimes had the feeling while reading *Love and Garbage* that I was reading *The Unbearable Lightness of Being* turned inside out. The rhetorical contrast between the two titles indicates just how discordant, even adversarial, the perspectives can be of imaginations engaged similarly with similar themes—in this case, with what Klíma's hero calls "the most important of all themes . . . suffering resulting from a life deprived of freedom."

During the early seventies, when I began to make a trip to Prague each spring, Ivan Klíma was my principal reality instructor. He drove me around to the street-corner kiosks where writers sold cigarettes, to the public buildings where they mopped the floors, to the construction sites where they were laying bricks, and out of the city to the municipal waterworks where they slogged about in overalls and boots, a wrench in one pocket and a book in the other. When I got to talk at length with these writers, it was often over dinner at Ivan's house.

After 1976 I was no longer able to get a visa to enter Czechoslovakia and we corresponded through the West German or Dutch couriers who discreetly carried manuscripts and books in and out of the country for the people who were under close surveillance. By the summer of 1978, ten years after the Russian invasion, even Ivan, who had always seemed to me the most effervescent of those I'd met in the opposition, was sufficiently exhausted to admit, in a letter written in somewhat uneven English, "Sometime I hesitate if it is reasonable to remain in this misery for the rest of our life." He went on:

> Our life here is not very encouraging—the abnormality lasts too long and is depressing. We are persecuted the whole time, it is not enough that we are not allowed to publish a single word in this country—we are asked for interrogations, many of my friends were arrested for the short time. I was not imprisoned, but I am deprived of my

driving license (without any reason of course) and my telephone is disconnected. But what is the worst: one of our colleagues . . .

Not uncharacteristically, he then described at much greater length a writer he considered to be in straits more dire than his own.

Fourteen years after I last saw him, Ivan Klíma's engaging blend of sprightliness and stolidness struck me as amazingly intact and his strength undiminished. Even though his Beatle haircut has been clipped back a bit since the seventies, his big facial features and mouthful of large carnivore teeth still make me sometimes think (particularly when he's having a good time) that I'm in the presence of a highly intellectually evolved Ringo Starr. Ivan had been at the center of the activities known now in Czechoslovakia as "the revolution," and yet he showed not the least sign of the exhaustion that even the young students reading English literature, whose Shakespeare class I sat in on at the university, told me had left them numb with fatigue and relieved to be back quietly studying even something as abstruse to them as the opening scenes of *Macbeth*.

I got a reminder of the stubborn force in Ivan's temperament during dinner at his house one evening as he advised a writer friend of his and mine how to go about getting back the tiny two-room apartment that had been confiscated by the authorities in the late seventies, when the friend had been hounded by the secret police into an impoverished exile. "Take your wife," Ivan told him, "take your four children, and go down to the office of Jaroslav Koran." Jaroslav Koran was the new mayor of Prague, formerly a translator of poetry from English; as the week passed and I either met or heard about Václav Havel's appointees, it began to seem to me as though a primary qualification for joining the new administration was having translated into Czech the poems of John Berryman. Have there ever before been so many translators, novelists, and poets at the head of anything other than the PEN club?

"In Koran's office," Ivan continued, "lie down on the floor, all of you, and refuse to move. Tell them, 'I'm a writer, they took my apartment, and I want it back.' Don't beg, don't complain, just lie there and refuse to move. You'll have an apartment in twenty-four hours." The writer without an apartment—a very spiritual and mild person who, since I'd seen him last selling cigarettes in Prague, had aged in all the ways that Ivan had not—responded only with a forlorn smile suggesting, gently, that Ivan was out of his mind. Ivan turned to me and said, matter-of-factly, "Some people don't have the stomach for this."

Helena Klímová, Ivan's wife, is a psychotherapist who received her training in the underground university that the dissidents conducted in various living rooms during the Russian occupation. When I asked how her patients were responding to the revolution and the new society it had ushered in, she told me, in her precise, affable, serious way, "The psychotics are getting better and the neurotics are getting worse." "How do you explain that?" I asked. "With all this new freedom," she said, "the neurotics are terribly uncertain. What will happen now? Nobody knows. The old rigidity was detestable, even to them, of course, but also reassuring, dependable. There was a structure. You knew what to expect and what not to expect. You knew whom to trust and whom to hate. To the neurotics the change is very unsettling. They are suddenly in a world of choices." "And the psychotics? Is it really possible that they're getting better?" "I think so, yes. The psychotics suck up the prevailing mood. Now it's exhilaration. Everybody is happy, so the psychotics are even happier. They are euphoric. It's all very strange. Everybody is suffering from adaptation shock."

I asked Helena what she was herself having most difficulty adapting to. Without hesitation she answered that it was all the people who were nice to her who never had been before—not that long ago she and Ivan had been treated most warily by neighbors and associates looking to avoid trouble. Helena's expression of anger over the rapidity with which those once so meticulously cautious—or outright censorious—people were now amicable to the Klímas was a surprise to me, since during their hardest years she had always impressed me as a marvel of tolerance and equilibrium. The psychotics were getting better, the neurotics were getting worse, and, despite the prevailing mood of exhilaration, among the bravely decent, the admirable handful, some were beginning openly to seethe a little with those poisoned emotions whose prudent management fortitude and sanity had demanded during the decades of resistance.

On my first full day in Prague, before Ivan came to meet me to begin our talks, I went for a morning walk on the shopping streets just off Václavské náměstí, the big open boulevard where the crowds that helped to chant the revolution through to success first assembled in November 1989. In only a few minutes, outside a storefront, I encountered a loose gathering of some seventy or eighty people, laughing at a voice coming over a loudspeaker. From the posters and inscriptions on the building I saw that, unwittingly, I had found the headquarters of Civic Forum, the opposition movement led by Havel.

This crowd of shoppers, strollers, and office workers was standing around together listening, as best I could figure out, to a comedian who must have been performing in an auditorium inside. I don't understand Czech, but I guessed that it was a comedian—and a very funny one—because the staccato rhythm of his monologue, the starts, stops, and shifts of tone, seemed consciously designed to provoke the crowd into spasms of laughter, which ripened into a rich roar and culminated, at the height of their hilarity, with outbursts of applause. It sounded like the response you hear from the audience at a Chaplin movie. I saw through a passageway that there was another laughing crowd of about the same size on the other side of the Civic Forum building. It was only when I crossed over to them that I understood what I was witnessing. On two television sets above the front window of Civic Forum was the comedian himself: viewed in close-up, seated alone at a conference table, was the former general secretary of the Czech Communist Party, Milos Jakes. Jakes, who'd been driven from office early in December 1989, was addressing a closed meeting of party apparatchiks in the industrial city of Pilsen in October.

I knew it was Jakes at the Pilsen meeting because the evening before, at dinner, Ivan and his son, Michal, had told me all about this videotape, which had been made secretly by the staff of Czech TV. Now it played continuously outside the Prague headquarters of Civic Forum, where passersby stopped throughout the day to have a good laugh. What they were laughing at was Jakes's dogmatic, humorless party rhetoric and his primitive, awkward Czech —the deplorably tangled sentences, the ludicrous malapropisms, the euphemisms and evasions and lies, the pure jerkish that, only months earlier, had filled so many people with shame and loathing. Michal had told me that on New Year's Eve Radio Free Europe had played Jakes's Pilsen videotape as "the funniest performance of the year."

Watching people walk back out into the street grinning, I thought that this must be the highest purpose of laughter, its sacramental reason for being—to bury wickedness in ridicule. It seemed a very hopeful sign that so many ordinary men and women (and teenagers, and even children, who were in the crowd) should be able to recognize that the offense against their language had been as humiliating and atrocious as anything else. Ivan told me later that at one point during the revolution a vast crowd had been addressed for a few minutes by a sympathetic young emissary from the Hungarian democratic movement, who concluded his remarks by apologizing to them for his imperfect Czech. Instantaneously, as one voice, a half million people roared back, "You speak better than Jakes."

Pasted to the window beneath the TV sets were two of the ubiquitous posters of the face of Václav Havel, whose Czech is everything that Jakes's is not.

Ivan Klíma and I spent our first two days together talking; then, in writing, we compressed the heart of our discussion into the exchange that follows.

Roth: What has it been like, all these years, publishing in your own country in samizdat editions? The surreptitious publication of serious literary works in small quantities must find an audience that is, generally speaking, more enlightened and intellectually more sophisticated than the wider Czech readership. Samizdat publication presumably fosters a solidarity between writer and reader that can be exhilarating. Yet because samizdat is a limited and artificial response to the evil of censorship, it remains unfulfilling for everyone. Tell me about the literary culture that was spawned here by samizdat publication.

Klíma: Your observation that samizdat literature fosters a special type of reader seems right. The Czech samizdat originated in a situation that is in its way unique. The Power, supported by foreign armies—the Power installed by the occupier and aware that it could exist only by the will of the occupier—was afraid of criticism. It also realized that any kind of spiritual life at all is directed in the end toward freedom. That's why it did not hesitate to forbid practically all Czech culture, to make it impossible for writers to write, painters to exhibit, scientists—especially in the social sciences—to carry out independent research; it destroyed the universities, appointing as professors for the most part docile clerks. The nation, caught unawares in this catastrophe, accepted it passively, at least for a time, looking on helplessly at the disappearance, one after another, of people whom it had so recently respected and to whom it had looked with hope.

Samizdat originated slowly. At the beginning of the seventies, my friends and fellow writers who were forbidden to publish used to meet at my house once a month. They included the leading creators of Czech literature: Václav Havel, Jiří Gruša, Ludvík Vaculík, Pavel Kohout, Alexandr Kliment, Jan Trefulka, Milan Uhde, and several dozen others. At these meetings we read our new work aloud to one another; some, like Bohumil Hrabal and Jaroslav Seifert, did not come personally but sent their work for us to read. The police got interested in these meetings; on their instructions television produced a short film that hinted darkly that dangerous conspiratorial conclaves were going on in my flat. I was told to cancel the meetings, but we all agreed that we would type out our manuscripts and sell them for the price of the copy. The "business" was taken on by one of the best Czech writers, Ludvík Vaculík. That's how we began, one typist and one ordinary typewriter.

The works were printed in editions of ten to twenty copies; the cost of one copy was about three times the price of a normal book. Soon what we were doing got about. People began to look out for these books. New "workshops" sprang up, which often copied the unauthorized copies. At the same time the standard of the layout improved. Somewhat deviously, we managed to have books bound at the state bookbindery; they were often accompanied by drawings by leading artists, also banned. Many of these books will be, or already are, the pride of bibliophiles' collections. As time went on, the numbers of copies increased, as did the titles and readers. Almost everyone "lucky" enough to own a samizdat was surrounded by a circle interested in borrowing it. The writers were soon followed by others: philosophers, historians, sociologists, nonconforming Catholics, as well as supporters of jazz, pop, and folk music, and young writers who refused to publish officially even though they were allowed to. Dozens of books in translation began to come out in this way, political books, religious books, often lyrical poetry or meditative prose. Whole editions came into being and remarkable feats of editing—for instance, the collected writings, with commentary, of our greatest contemporary philosopher, Jan Patocka.

At first the police tried to prevent samizdats, confiscating individual copies during house searches. A couple of times they arrested the typists who copied them, and some were even sentenced to imprisonment by the "free" courts, but the samizdat started to resemble, from the point of view of the authorities, the many-headed dragon in the fairy tale, or a plague. Samizdat was unconquerable.

There are no precise statistics yet, but I know there were roughly two hundred samizdat periodicals alone and several thousand books. Of course when we speak of thousands of book titles we can't always expect high quality, but one thing completely separated samizdat from the rest of Czech culture: it was independent both of the market and of the censor. This independent Czech culture strongly attracted the younger generation, in part because it had the aura of the forbidden. How widespread it really was will perhaps soon be answered by scientific research; we've estimated that some books had tens of thousands of readers, and we mustn't forget that a lot of these books were published by Czech publishing houses in exile and then returned to Czechoslovakia by the most devious routes.

Nor should we pass over the great part played in propagating what was called "uncensored literature" by the foreign broadcasting stations Radio Free Europe and the Voice of America. Radio Free Europe broadcast the most important of the samizdat books in serial form, and its listeners numbered in the hundreds of thousands. (One of the last books that I heard read on this station was Havel's remarkable *Long-Distance Interrogation*, which is an account not only of his life but also of his political ideas.) I'm convinced that this "underground culture" had an important influence on the revolutionary events of the autumn of 1989.

Roth: It always seemed to me that there was a certain amount of loose, romantic talk in the West about "the muse of censorship" behind the Iron Curtain. I would venture that there were even writers in the West who sometimes envied the terrible pressure under which you people wrote and the clarity of the mission this burden fostered: in your society you were virtually the only monitors of truth. In a censorship culture, where everybody lives a double life—of lies and truth—literature becomes a life preserver, the remnant of truth people cling to. I think it's also true that in a culture like mine, where nothing is censored but where the mass media inundate us with inane falsifications of human affairs, serious literature is no less of a life preserver, even if the society is all but oblivious of it.

When I returned to the United States from Prague after my first visit in the early seventies, I compared the Czech writers' situation to ours in America by saying, "There nothing goes and everything matters; here everything goes and nothing matters." But at what cost did everything you wrote matter so much? How would you estimate the toll that repression, which put such a high premium on literature, has taken on the writers you know?

Klíma: Your comparison of the situation of Czech writers and writers in a free country is one that I have often repeated. I'm not able to judge the paradox of the second half, but the first catches the paradox of our situation wonderfully. Writers had to pay a high price for these words that take on importance because of the bans and persecution—the ban on publishing was connected not only to a ban on all social activity but also, in most cases, to a ban on doing any work writers were qualified for. Almost all my banned colleagues had to earn their living as laborers. Window cleaners, as we know them from Kundera's novel [*The Unbearable Lightness of Being*], were not really typical among doctors, but there were many writers, critics, and translators who earned their living in this way. Others worked on the building sites of the underground, as crane operators, or digging at geological research sites. Now, it might seem that such work could provide an interesting experience for a writer. And that's true, so long as the work lasts for a limited time and there is some prospect of escape from blunting and exhausting drudgery. Fifteen or even twenty years of work like that, exclusion like that, affects one's whole personality. The cruelty and injustice completely broke some of those subjected to it; others were so exhausted that they were simply unable to undertake any creative work. If they did somehow manage to persevere, it was by sacrificing to this work everything: any claim to rest and often to any chance of a personal life.

Roth: Milan Kundera, I discover, is something of an obsession here among the writers and journalists I talk to. There appears to be a controversy over what might be called his "internationalism." Some people have suggested to me that, in his two books written in exile, *The Book of Laughter and Forgetting* and *The Unbearable Lightness of Being,* he is writing "for" the French, "for" the Americans, and so on, and that this constitutes some sort of cultural misdemeanor or even betrayal. To me he seems rather to be a writer who, once he found himself living abroad, decided, quite realistically, that it was best not to pretend that he was a writer living at home, and who had then to devise for himself a literary strategy, one congruent not with his old but with his new complexities. Leaving aside the matter of quality, the marked difference of approach between the books written in Czechoslovakia, like *The Joke* and *Laughable Loves,* and those written in France does not represent to me a lapse of integrity, let alone a falsification of his experience, but a strong, innovative response to an inescapable challenge. Would you explain what problems Kundera presents to those Czech intellectuals who are so obsessed with his writing in exile?

Klíma: Their relation to Kundera is indeed complicated, and I would stress beforehand that only a minority of Czechs have any opinion about Kundera's writing, for one simple reason: his books have not been published in Czechoslovakia for more than twenty years. The reproach that he is writing for foreigners rather than for Czechs is only one of the many reproaches addressed to Kundera and only a part of the more substantial rebuke—that he has lost his ties to his native country. We can really leave aside the matter of quality because largely the allergy to him is not produced by the quality of his writing but by something else.

The defenders of Kundera—and there are many here—explain the animosity toward him among Czech intellectuals by what is not so rare an attitude toward our famous Czech compatriots: envy. But I don't see this problem so simply. I can mention many famous compatriots, even among the writers (Havel at home, Skvorecký abroad), who are very popular and even beloved by intellectuals here.

I have used the word *allergy*. Various irritants produce an allergy, and it's rather difficult to find the crucial ones. In my opinion the allergy is caused, in part, by what people take to be the simplified and spectacular way in which Kundera presents his Czech experience. What's more, the experience he presents is, they would say, at odds with the fact that he himself was an indulged and rewarded child of the Communist regime until 1968.

The totalitarian system is terribly hard on people, as

Kundera recognizes, but the hardness of life has a much more complicated shape than we find in his presentation of it. Kundera's picture, his critics would tell you, is the sort of picture that you would see from a very capable foreign journalist who'd spent a few days in our country. Such a picture is acceptable to the Western reader because it confirms his expectations; it reinforces the fairy tale about good and evil, which a good child likes to hear again and again. But for these Czech readers our reality is no fairy tale. They expect a much more comprehensive and complex picture, a deeper insight into our lives from a writer of Kundera's stature. Kundera certainly has other aspirations for his writing than only to give a picture of Czech reality, but those attributes of his work may not be so relevant for the Czech audience I'm talking about.

Another reason for the allergy probably has to do with the prudery of some Czech readers. Although in their personal lives they may not behave puritanically, they are rather more strict about an author's morality.

Last but not least is an extraliterary reason, which may, however, be at the very core of the charge against him. At the time when Kundera was achieving his greatest world popularity, Czech culture was in a bitter struggle with the totalitarian system. Intellectuals at home as well as those in exile shared in this struggle. They underwent all sorts of hardships: they sacrificed their personal freedom, their professional positions, their time, their comfortable lives. For example, Josef Skvorecký and his wife virtually abandoned their personal lives to work from abroad on behalf of suppressed Czech literature. Kundera seems to many people to have stood apart from this kind of effort. Surely it was Kundera's right—why should every writer have to become a fighter?—and it certainly can be argued that he has done more than enough for the Czech cause by his writing itself. Anyway, I have tried to explain to you, quite candidly, why Kundera has been accepted in his own country with considerably more hesitation than in the rest of the world.

In his defense, let me say that there is a kind of xenophobia here with respect to the suffering of the last half century. The Czechs are by now rather possessive of their suffering, and though this is perhaps understandable and a natural enough deformation, it has resulted, in my opinion, in an unjust denigration of Kundera, who is, without a doubt, one of the great Czech writers of this century.

Roth: The official, or officialized, writers are a bit of a mystery to me. Were they all bad writers? Were there any interesting opportunistic writers? I say opportunistic writers rather than believing writers because, though there may well have been believers among the writers in the first decade or so after World War II, I assume that during the past decade the official writers were opportunists and nothing more. Correct me if I'm wrong about that. And then tell me, was it possible to remain a good writer and accept the official rulers and their rules? Or was the work automatically weakened and compromised by this acceptance?

Klíma: It's quite true that there is a basic difference between authors who supported the regime in the fifties and those who supported it after the occupation in 1968. Before the war, what was called leftist literature played a relatively important role. The fact that the Soviet army liberated the greater part of the republic further strengthened this leftist tendency; so did the memory of Munich and the Western powers' desertion of Czechoslovakia, despite all their treaties and promises. The younger generation especially succumbed to illusions of a new and more just society that the Communists were going to build. It was precisely this generation that soon saw through the regime and contributed enormously to setting off the '68 Prague Spring movement and to demystifying the Stalinist dictatorship.

After 1968 there was no longer any reason for anyone, except perhaps a few frenzied fanatics, to share those postwar illusions. The Soviet army had changed in the eyes of the nation from a liberating army to an army of occupation, and the regime that supported this occupation had changed into a band of collaborators. If a writer didn't notice these changes, his blindness deprived him of the right to count himself among creative spirits; if he noticed them but pretended he knew nothing about them, we may rightfully call him an opportunist—it is probably the kindest word we can use.

Of course the problem lay in the fact that the regime did not last just a few months or years but two decades. This meant that, exceptions apart—and the regime persecuted these exceptions harshly—virtually a generation of protesters, from the end of the seventies on, was hounded into emigration. Everyone else had to accept the regime in some way or even support it. Television and radio had to function somehow, the publishing houses had to cover paper with print. Even quite decent people thought, "If I don't hold this job, someone worse will. If I do not write—and I shall try to smuggle at least a bit of truth through to the reader—the only people left will be those who are willing to serve the regime devotedly and uncritically."

I want to avoid saying that everyone who published anything over the past twenty years is necessarily a bad writer. It's true too that the regime gradually tried to make some important Czech writers their own and so began to publish some of their works. In this way it published at least a few works by Bohumil Hrabal and the poet Miroslav Holub (both of them made public self-criticisms) and also poems by the Nobel Prize winner Jaroslav Seifert, who signed Charter 77. But it can be stated categorically that the effort of publication, getting past all the traps laid by the censor, was a severe burden on the works of many of those who were published. I have carefully compared the works of Hrabal—who, to my mind, is one of the greatest living European prose writers—that came out in samizdat form and were published abroad and those that were published officially in Czechoslovakia. The changes he was evidently forced to make by the censor are, from the point of view of the work, monstrous in the true sense of the word. But much worse than this was the fact that many writers reckoned with censorship beforehand and deformed their own work, and so, of course, deformed themselves.

Only in the eighties did "angry young men" begin to appear, especially among young writers, theater people, and the authors of protest songs. They said exactly what they meant and risked their works not coming out or even losing their livelihoods. They contributed to our having a free literature today—and not only literature.

Roth: Since the Soviet occupation of Czechoslovakia a sizable sampling of contemporary Czech writers have been published in the United States: from among those living in exile, Kundera, Pavel Kohout, Skvorecký, Jirí Grusa, and Arnost Lustig; from among those in Czechoslovakia, you, Vaculík, Hrabal, Holub, and Havel. This is an astonishing representation from a small European country—I, for one, can't think of ten Norwegian or ten Dutch writers who have been published in America since 1968. To be sure, the place that produced Kafka has special significance, but I don't think either of us believes that this accounts for the attention that your nation's literature has been able to command in the West. You have had the ear of many foreign writers. They have been incredibly deferential to your literature. You have been given a special hearing and your lives and works have absorbed a lot of their thinking. Has it occurred to you that this has now all changed and that in the future you're perhaps going to be talking not so much to us but to one another again?

Klíma: Certainly the harsh fate of the nation, as we have said, suggested many compelling themes. A writer was himself often forced by circumstances to have experiences that would otherwise have remained foreign to him and that, when he wrote about them, may have appeared to readers almost exotic. It's also true that writing—or work in the arts altogether—was the last place where one could still set up shop as an individual. Many creative people actually became writers just for this reason. All this will pass to some extent, even though I think that there is an aversion to the cult of the elite in Czech society and that Czech writers will always be concerned with the everyday problems of ordinary people. This applies to the great writers of the past as well as to contemporary ones: Kafka never ceased to be an office worker or Capek a journalist; Hasek and Hrabal spent a lot of their time in smoky pubs with beer-drinking buddies. Holub never left his job as a scientist and Vaculík stubbornly avoided everything that might drag him away from leading the life of the most ordinary of citizens. Of course as changes come in social life, so will changes in themes. But I'm not sure this will mean our literature will necessarily become uninteresting to outsiders. I believe that our literature has pushed open the gate to Europe and even to the world just a crack, not only because of its subject but because of its quality too.

Roth: And inside Czechoslovakia? Right now I know people are wildly hungry for books, but after the revolutionary fervor subsides, with the sense of unity in struggle dissipating, might you not come to mean far less to readers here than you did when you were fighting to keep alive for them a language other than that of the official newspapers, the official speeches, and the official government-sanctioned books?

Klíma: I agree that our literature will lose some of its extraliterary appeal. But many think that these secondary appeals were distracting both writers and readers with questions that should really have been answered by journalists, by sociologists, by political analysts. Let's go back to what I call the intriguing plots offered by the totalitarian system. Stupidity triumphant, the arrogance of power, violence against the innocent, police brutality, the ruthlessness that permeates life and produces labor camps and prisons, the humiliation of man, life based on lies and pretenses—these stories will lose their topicality, I hope, even though writers will probably return to consider them again after a while. But the new situation must bring new subjects. In the first place, forty years of the totalitarian system have left behind a material and spiritual emptiness, and filling this emptiness will involve difficulties, tension, disappointment, and tragedy.

It is also true that in Czechoslovakia a feeling for books has a deep tradition, reaching back to the Middle Ages, and even with television sets everywhere, it's hard to find a family that does not own a library of good books. Even though I don't like prophesying, I believe that at least for now the fall of the totalitarian system will not turn literature into an occasional subject with which to ward off boredom at parties.

Roth: The Polish writer Tadeusz Borowski said that the only way to write about the Holocaust was as the guilty, as the complicit and implicated; that is what he did in his first-person fictional memoir, *This Way for the Gas, Ladies and Gentlemen.* There Borowski may even have pretended to a dramatically more chilling degree of moral numbness than he felt as an Auschwitz prisoner, precisely to reveal the Auschwitz horror as the wholly innocent victims could not. Under the domination of Soviet Communism, some of the most original Eastern European writers I have read in English have positioned themselves similarly—Tadeusz Konwicki, Danilo Kiš, and Kundera, say, to name only three K's, who have crawled out from under Kafka's cockroach to tell us that there are no uncontaminated angels, that the evil is inside as well as outside. Still, this sort of self-flagellation, despite its ironies and nuances, cannot be free from the element of blame, from the moral habit of situating the source of the evil in the system even when examining how the system contaminates you and me. You are used to being on the side of truth, with all the risks entailed in becoming righteous, pious, didactic, dutifully counterpropagandistic. You are not used to living without that well-defined, recognizable, objective sort of evil. I wonder what will happen to your writing—and to the moral habits embedded in it—with the removal of the system: without them, with just you and me.

Klíma: That question makes me think back over everything I have said until now. I have found that I often do describe a conflict in which I am defending myself against an aggressive world, embodied by the system. But I have often written about the conflict between the system and me without necessarily supposing that the world is worse than I am. I should say that the dichotomy, I on the one side and the world on the other, is the way in which not only writers but all of us are tempted to perceive things.

Whether the world appears as a bad system or as bad individuals, bad laws, or bad luck is not really the point. We could both name dozens of works created in free societies in which the hero is flung here and there by a bad, hostile, misunderstanding society, and so assure each other that it is not only in our part of the world that writers succumb to the temptation to see the conflict between themselves—or their heroes—and the world around them as the dualism of good and evil.

I would imagine that those here in the habit of seeing the world dualistically will certainly be able to find some other form of external evil. On the other hand, the changed situation could help others to step out of the cycle of merely reacting to the cruelty or stupidity of the system and lead them to reflect anew on man in the world. And what will happen to my writing now? Over the past three months I have been swamped with so many other duties that the idea that someday I'll write a story in peace and quiet seems to me fantastic. But not to evade the question—for my writing, the fact that I shall no longer have to worry about the unhappy social system I regard as a relief.

Roth: Kafka. Last November, while the demonstrations that resulted in the new Czechoslovakia were being addressed by the outcast ex-convict Havel here in Prague, I was teaching a course on Kafka at a college in New York City. The students read *The Castle*, about K.'s tedious, fruitless struggle to gain recognition as a land surveyor from that mighty and inaccessible sleepyhead who controls the castle bureaucracy, Mr. Klamm. When the photograph appeared in the *New York Times* showing Havel reaching across a conference table to shake the hand of the old regime's prime minister, I showed it to my class. "Well," I said, "K. meets Klamm at last." The students were pleased when Havel decided to run for president—that would put K. in the castle, and as successor, no less, to Klamm's boss.

Kafka's prescient irony may not be the most remarkable attribute of his work, but it's always stunning to think about it. He is anything but a fantasist creating a dream or a nightmare world as opposed to a realistic one. His fiction keeps insisting that what seems to be unimaginable hallucination and hopeless paradox is precisely what constitutes one's reality. In works like "The Metamorphosis," *The Trial*, and *The Castle*, he chronicles the education of someone who comes to accept—rather too late, in the case of the accused Joseph K.—that what looks to be outlandish and ludicrous and unbelievable, beneath your dignity and concern, is nothing less than what is happening to you: that thing beneath your dignity turns out to be your destiny.

"It was no dream," Kafka writes only moments after Gregor Samsa awakens to discover that he is no longer a good son supporting his family but a repellent insect. The *dream*, according to Kafka, is of a world of probability, of proportion, of stability and order, of cause and effect—a dependable world of dignity and justice is what is absurdly fantastic to him. How amused Kafka would have been by the indignation of those dreamers who tell us daily, "I didn't come here to be insulted!" In Kafka's world—and not just in Kafka's world—life begins to make sense only when we realize that that is why we *are* here.

I'd like to know what role Kafka may have played in your imagination during your years of being here to be insulted. Kafka was banned by the Communist authorities from the bookstores, libraries, and universities in his own city and throughout Czechoslovakia. Why? What frightened them? What enraged them? What did he mean to the rest of you who know his work intimately and may even feel a strong affinity with his origins?

Klíma: Like you, I have studied Kafka's works—not too long ago I wrote an extensive essay about him and a play about his love affair with Felice Bauer. I would formulate my opinion on the conflict between the dream world and the real one in his work just a little bit differently. You say: "The dream, according to Kafka, is of a world of probability, of proportion, of stability and order, of cause and effect—a dependable world of dignity and justice is what is absurdly fantastic to him." I would replace the word *fantastic* with the word *unattainable.* What you call the dream world was rather for Kafka the real world, the world in which order reigned, in which people, at least as he saw it, were able to grow fond of one another, make love, have families, be orderly in all their duties—but this world was for him, with his almost sick truthfulness, unattainable. His heroes suffered not because they were unable to realize their dream but because they were not strong enough to enter properly into the real world, to properly fulfill their duty.

The question why Kafka was banned under Communist regimes is answered in a single sentence by the hero of my novel *Love and Garbage:* "What matters most about Kafka's personality is his honesty." A regime that is built on deception, that asks people to pretend, that demands external agreement without caring about the inner conviction of those to whom it turns for consent, a regime afraid of anyone who asks about the sense of his action, cannot allow anyone whose veracity attained such fascinating or even terrifying completeness to speak to the people.

If you ask what Kafka meant for me, we get back to the question we somehow keep circling. On the whole Kafka was an unpolitical writer. I like to quote the entry in his diary for August 21, 1914. It is very short. "Germany has declared war on Russia.—Swimming in the afternoon." Here the historic, world-shaking plane and the personal one are exactly level. I am sure that Kafka wrote only from his innermost need to confess his personal crises and so solve what was for him insoluble in his personal life—in the first place his relationship with his father and his inability to pass beyond a certain limit in his relationships with women. In my essay on Kafka I show that, for instance, his murderous machine in the short story "In the Penal Colony" is a wonderful, passionate, and desperate image of the state of being married or engaged. Several years after writing this story he confided to Milena Jesenska his feelings on thinking about their living together:

> You know, when I try to write down something [about our engagement] the swords whose points surround me in a circle begin slowly to approach the body, it's the most complete torture; when they begin to graze me it's already so terrible that I immediately at the first scream betray you, myself, everything.

Kafka's metaphors were so powerful that they far exceeded his original intentions. I know that *The Trial* as well as "In the Penal Colony" have been explained as ingenious prophesies of the terrible fate that befell the Jewish nation during World War II, which broke out fifteen years after Kafka's death. But it was no prophecy of genius. These works merely prove that a creator who knows how to reflect his most personal experiences deeply and truthfully also touches the suprapersonal or social spheres. Again I am answering the question about political content in literature. Literature doesn't have to scratch around for political realities or even worry about systems that come and go; it can transcend them and still answer questions that the system evokes in people. This is the most important lesson that I extracted for myself from Kafka.

Roth: Ivan, you were born a Jew and, because you were a Jew, you spent part of your childhood in a concentration camp. Do you feel that this background distinguishes your work—or that, under the Communists, it altered your predicament as a writer—in ways worth talking about? In the decade before the war, Central Europe without Jews as a pervasive cultural presence—without Jewish readers or Jewish writers, without Jewish journalists, playwrights, publishers, critics—was unthinkable. Now that the literary life in this part of Europe is about to be conducted once again in an intellectual atmosphere that harks back to prewar days, I wonder if—perhaps even for the first time—the absence of Jews will register with any impact on the society. Is there a remnant left in Czech literature of the prewar Jewish culture, or have the mentality and sensibility of Jews, which were once strong in Prague, left Czech literature for good?

Klíma: Anyone who has been through a concentration camp as a child—who has been completely dependent on an external power that can at any moment come in and beat or kill him and everyone around him—probably moves through life at least a bit differently from people who have been spared such an education. That life can be snapped like a piece of string—that was my daily lesson as a child. And the effect of this on my writing? An obsession with the problem of justice, with the feelings of people who have been condemned and cast out, the lonely and the helpless. The themes issuing from this, thanks to the fate of my country, have lost nothing of their topicality. And the effect on my life? Among friends I have always been known as an optimist. Anyone who survives being repeatedly condemned to death may suffer either from paranoia all his life or from a confidence not justified by reason that everything can be survived and everything will turn out all right in the end.

As for the influence of Jewish culture on our present culture—if we look back, we are apt to idealize the cultural reality in rather the same way that we idealize our own childhoods. If I look back at my native Prague, say at the beginning of this century, I am amazed by the marvelous mix of cultures and customs, by the city's many great men. Kafka, Rilke, Hasek, Werfel, Einstein, Dvořák, Max Brod . . . But of course the past of Prague, which I name here only as a symbol of Central Europe, consisted not only of a dazzling number of the greatly gifted, not only of a culture surge; it was also a time of hatred, of furious and petty and often bloody clashes.

If we speak of the magnificent surge of Jewish culture that Prague witnessed more than almost anywhere else, we must recognize also that there has never been a long period here without some sort of anti-Semitic explosion. To most people the Jews represented a foreign element, which they tried at the very least to isolate. There is no doubt that

Jewish culture enriched Czech culture, by the very fact that, like German culture, which also had an important presence in Bohemia—and Jewish literature in Bohemia was largely written in German—it became for the developing Czech culture, whose evolution had been stifled for two hundred years, a bridge to Western Europe.

What has survived from that past? Seemingly nothing. But I'm convinced this is not the whole story. The present longing to overcome the nihilist past with tolerance, the longing to return to untainted sources, is this not a response to the almost forgotten warning call of the dead, and indeed the murdered, to us, the living?

Roth: Havel. A complicated man of mischievous irony and solid intellect like Havel, a man of letters, a student of philosophy, an idealist with strong spiritual inclinations, a playful thinker who speaks his native language with precision and directness, who reasons with logic and nuance, who laughs with gusto, who is enchanted with theatricality, who knows intimately and understands his country's history and culture—such a person would have even less chance of being elected president in America than Jesse Jackson or Geraldine Ferraro.

Just this morning I went to the Castle, to a press conference Havel held about his trips to the United States and Russia, and I listened with pleasure and some astonishment to a president composing, on the spot, sentences that were punchy, fluent, and rich with human observation, sentences of a kind that probably haven't been formulated so abundantly—and off the cuff—at our White House since Lincoln was shot.

When a German journalist asked whose company Havel had most preferred, the Dalai Lama's, George Bush's, or Mikhail Gorbachev's—all three of whom he's recently met

—he began, "Well, it wouldn't be wise to make a hierarchy of sympathy . . ." When asked to describe Gorbachev, he said that one of Gorbachev's most attractive qualities is that "he is a man who doesn't hesitate to confess his embarrassment when he feels it." When he announced that he had scheduled the arrival of the West German president for March 15—the same day Hitler entered Prague in 1939—one of the reporters noted that Havel "liked anniversaries," whereupon Havel immediately corrected him. "No," he told him, "I did not say that I 'liked anniversaries.' I spoke about symbols, metaphors, and a sense of dramatic structures in politics."

How did this happen here? And why did it happen here to Havel? As he would probably be the first to recognize, he was not the only stubborn, outspoken person among you, nor was he alone imprisoned for his ideas. I'd like you to tell me why he has emerged as the embodiment of this nation's new idea of itself. I wonder if he was quite such a hero to large segments of the nation when, altogether quixotically—the very epitome of the foolish, high-minded intellectual who doesn't understand real life—he was writing long, seemingly futile letters of protest to his predecessor, President Husak. Didn't a lot of people think of him then as either a nuisance or a nut? For the hundreds of thousands who never really raised an objection to the Communist regime, isn't worshiping Havel a convenient means by which to jettison, practically overnight, their own complicity with what you call the nihilist past?

Klíma: Before I try to explain that remarkable phenomenon "Havel," I'll try to give my opinion on the personality named Havel. (I hope I won't be breaking the law, still extant, that virtually forbids criticism of the president.) I agree with your characterization of Havel. Only, as someone who has met him innumerable times over the past twenty-five years, I would supplement it. Havel is mainly known to the world as an important dramatist, then as an interesting essayist, and lastly as a dissident, an opponent of the regime so firm in his principles that he did not hesitate to undergo anything for his convictions, including a Czech prison—more exactly, a Communist prison. But in this list of Havel's skills or professions there is one thing missing, and in my opinion it's the fundamental one.

As a dramatist Havel is placed by world critics in the stream of the theater of the absurd. But back when it was still permissible to present Havel's plays in our theaters, the Czech public understood them primarily as political plays. I used to say, half jokingly, that Havel became a dramatist simply because at that time the theater was the only platform from which political opinions could be expressed. Right from the beginning, when I got to know him, Havel was, for me, in the first place a politician, in the second place an essayist of genius, and only last a dramatist. I am not ordering the value of his achievements but rather the priority of interest, personal inclination, and enthusiasm.

In the Czech political desert, where former representatives of the democratic regime had either emigrated, been locked up, or had completely disappeared from the political scene, Havel was for a long time really the only active representative of the line of thoroughly democratic Czech politics represented by Tomáš Masaryk. Today Masaryk lives in the national consciousness rather as an idol or as the author of the principles on which the First Republic was built. Few people know that he was an outstanding politician, a master of compromises and surprising political moves, of risky, ethically motivated acts. (One of these was the passionate defense of a poor, wandering young Jew from a well-to-do family, Leopold Hossner, who was accused and convicted of the ritual murder of a young dressmaker. This act of Masaryk's so enraged the Czech nationalist public that it looked for a while as if the experienced politician had committed political suicide—he must then have seemed to his contemporaries to be "a nuisance or a nut.") Havel brilliantly continued in Masaryk's line of "suicidal" ethical behavior, though of course he carried on his political activity under much more formidable conditions than those of old Austria-Hungary. His letter to Husak in 1975 was indeed an ethically motivated but expressly political—even suicidal—act, just like the signature campaigns that he instigated over and over again, for which he was always persecuted.

Like Masaryk, Havel was a master of compromises and alliances who never lost sight of the basic aim: to remove the totalitarian system and replace it with a renewed system of pluralist democracy. For that aim he did not hesitate in 1977 to join together all the antitotalitarian forces, whether they were reform Communists—all of them long since expelled from the party—members of the arts underground, or believing Christians. The greatest significance of Charter 77 lay precisely in this unifying act, and I haven't the slightest doubt that it was Václav Havel himself who was the author of this conception and that his was the personality that was able to link such absolutely heterogeneous political forces.

Havel's candidacy for president and his election were, in the first place, an expression of the precipitate, truly revolutionary course of events in this country. When I was returning from a meeting of one of the committees of Civic Forum one day toward the end of last November, my friends and I were saying to one another that the time was near when we should nominate our candidate for the office of president. We agreed then that the only candidate to consider, for he enjoyed the relatively wide support of the public, was Alexander Dubček. But it became clear a few days later that the revolution had gone beyond the point where any candidate who was connected, if only by his past, with the Communist Party was acceptable to the younger generation of Czechs. At that moment the only suitable candidate emerged—Václav Havel. Again it was an example of Havel's political instincts—and Dubček certainly remained the only suitable candidate for Slovakia—that he linked his candidacy with the condition that Dubček should be given the second-highest function in the state.

I explain the change of attitude toward him by the Czech public—because for a certain sector here Havel was, indeed, more or less unknown, or known as the son of a rich capitalist and even as a convict—by the revolutionary ethos that seized the nation. In a certain atmosphere, in the midst of a crowd, however civil and restrained the crowd may be, an individual suddenly identifies himself with the prevailing mood and state of mind and captures the crowd's enthusiasm. It's true that the majority of the country shared in the doings of the former system, but it's also true that the majority hated it at the same time just because it had made them complicit in its awfulness, and hardly anyone identified himself any longer with that regime which had so often humiliated, deceived, and cheated them. Within a few days Havel became the symbol of revolutionary change, the man who would lead society out of its crisis—nobody had any exact idea how—lead it out of evil to good. Whether the motivation for supporting him was basically metaphysical, whether this support will be maintained or eventually come to be based more on reason and practical concerns, time will tell.

Roth: Earlier we spoke about the future. May I close with a prophecy of my own? What I say may strike you as arrogantly patronizing—the freedom-rich man warning the freedom-poor man about the dangers of becoming rich. You have fought for something for so many years now, something that you needed like air, and what I am going to say is that the air you fought for is poisoned a little too. I assure you that I am not a sacred artist putting down the profane nor am I a poor little rich boy whining about his luxuries. I am not complaining. I am only making a report to the academy.

There is still a pre–World War II varnish on the societies that, since the forties, have been under Soviet domination. The countries of the satellite world have been caught in a time warp, with the result, for instance, that the McLuhanite revolution has barely touched your lives. Prague is still very much Prague and not a part of the global village. Czechoslovakia is still Czechoslovakia, and yet the Europe you are rejoining is a rapidly homogenizing Europe, a Europe whose very distinct nations are on the brink of being radically transformed. You live here in a society of prelapsarian racial innocence, knowing nothing of the great postcolonial migrations—your society, to my eyes, is astonishingly white. And then there is money and the culture of money that takes over in a market economy.

What are you going to do about money, you writers, about coming out from under the wing of a subsidized writers' union, a subsidized publishing industry, and competing in the marketplace and publishing profitable books? And what of this market economy that your new government is talking about—five, ten years from now, what are you going to make of the commercialized culture that it breeds?

As Czechoslovakia becomes a free, democratic consumer society, you writers are going to find yourselves bedeviled by a number of new adversaries from which, strangely enough, repressive, sterile totalitarianism protected you. Particularly unsettling will be the one adversary that is the pervasive, all-powerful archenemy of literature, literacy, and language. I can guarantee you that no defiant crowds will ever rally in Wenceslas Square to overthrow its tyranny nor will any playwright-intellectual be elevated by the outraged masses to redeem the national soul from the fatuity into which this adversary reduces virtually all of human discourse. I am speaking about that trivializer of everything, commercial television—not a handful of channels nobody wants to watch because it is controlled by an oafish state censor but a dozen or two channels of boring clichéd television that most everybody watches all the time because it is *entertaining*. At long last you and your writer colleagues have broken out of the intellectual prison of Communist totalitarianism. Welcome to the World of Total Entertainment. You don't know what you've been missing. Or do you?

Klíma: As a man who has, after all, lived for some time in the United States, and who for twenty years has been published only in the West, I am aware of the "danger" that a free society, and especially a market mechanism, brings to culture. Of course I know that most people prefer virtually any sort of kitsch to Cortázar or Hrabal. I know that the period will probably pass when even books of poetry in our country reach editions of tens of thousands. I suppose that a wave of literary and television garbage will break over our market—we can hardly prevent it. Nor am I alone in realizing that, in its newly won freedom, culture not only gains something important but also loses something. At the beginning of January one of our best Czech film directors was interviewed on television, and he gave a warning against the commercialization of culture. When he said that the censorship had protected us not only from the best works of our own and foreign culture but also from the worst of mass culture, he annoyed many people, but I understood him. A memorandum on the position of television recently appeared that states that

> television, owing to its widespread influence, is directly able to contribute to the greatest extent toward a moral revival. This of course presupposes . . . setting up a new structure, and not only in an organizational sense but in the sense of the moral and creative responsibility of the institution as a whole and of every single member of its staff, especially its leading ones. The times we are living through offer our television a unique chance to try for something that does not exist elsewhere in the world.

The memorandum does not of course ask for the introduction of censorship, but of a supraparty arts council, a group of independent authorities of the highest spiritual and moral standards. I signed this memorandum as the president of the Czech PEN club, although personally, for myself, I thought that the desire to structure the TV of a free society in this way was rather utopian. The language of the memorandum struck me as the kind of unrealistic and moralistic language that can emerge from the euphoria of revolution.

I have mentioned that, among intellectuals especially,

utopian ideas have begun to surface about how this country will link the good points of both systems—something from the state-controlled system, something from the new market system. And these ideas are probably strongest in the realm of culture. The future will show to what extent they are purely utopian. Will there be commercial television in our country, or will we continue only with subsidized, centrally directed broadcasting? And if this last does remain, will it manage to resist the demands of mass taste? We'll know only in time.

I have already told you that in Czechoslovakia literature has always enjoyed not only popularity but esteem. This is borne out by the fact that in a country with fewer than twelve million inhabitants, books by good writers, both Czech and translated, were published in editions of hundreds of thousands. What's more, the system is changing in our country at a time when ecological thinking is growing tremendously (the environment in Czechoslovakia is one of the worst in Europe), and it surely makes no sense for us to strive to purify the environment and at the same time to pollute our culture. So it is not really such a utopian idea to try to influence the mass media to maintain standards and even educate the nation. If at least some part of that idea could be realized, it would certainly be, as the authors of the memorandum say, a unique event in the history of mass communications. And after all, impulses of a spiritual character really have, from time to time, come from this little country of ours in the center of Europe.

Isaac Bashevis Singer

[1976]

SOME MONTHS after I first read Bruno Schulz and decided to include him in the Penguin series "Writers from the Other Europe," I learned that when his autobiographical novel, *The Street of Crocodiles,* appeared in English fourteen years ago, it had been reviewed and praised by Isaac Bashevis Singer. Since Schulz and Singer were born in Poland of Jewish parents within twelve years of each other—Schulz in 1892 in the provincial Galician city of Drohobycz, Singer in Radzymin, near Warsaw, in 1904—I telephoned Singer, whom I had met socially once or twice, and asked if we might get together to talk about Schulz and about what life had been like for a Jewish writer in Poland during the decades when they were both coming of age there as artists. Our meeting took place in Singer's Manhattan apartment at the end of November 1976.

Roth: When did you first read Schulz, here or in Poland?
Singer: I read him in the United States for the first time. I must tell you, like many another writer I approach a book of fiction always with some kind of doubts; since the major-

ity of writers are not really good writers, I assume when I am sent a book that it's going to be not too good a book. And I was surprised the moment I began to read Schulz. I said to myself, here is a first-class writer.

Roth: Had you known Schulz's name before?

Singer: No, I didn't even know Schulz's name. I left Poland in 1935. Schulz was not really known then—and if he was known, I didn't know about him. I never heard of him. My first impression was that this man writes like Kafka. There are two writers about whom they say they write like Kafka. One was Agnon. Agnon used to say that he never read Kafka, but people have some doubts about it. As a matter of fact he did read Kafka, there is no question about it. I wouldn't say he was influenced by Kafka; there is a possibility that two or three people write in the same kind of style, in the same spirit. Because not every person is completely unique. If God could create one Kafka, He could have created three Kafkas, if He was in the mood to do so. But the more I read Schulz—maybe I shouldn't say it— but when I read him, I said he's better than Kafka. There is greater strength in some of his stories. Also he's very strong in the absurd, though not in a silly way but in a clever way. I would say that between Schulz and Kafka there is something that Goethe calls *Wahlverwandtschaft,* an affinity of souls that you have chosen for yourself. This might have been the case completely with Schulz, and it might also be to a degree with Agnon.

Roth: To me it seems as though Schulz could not keep his imagination away from anything, including the work of other writers, and particularly the work of someone like Kafka, with whom he does seem to have had important affinities of background and temperament. Just as in *The*

Street of Crocodiles he reimagines his hometown of Drohobycz into a more terrifying and wonderful place than it
actually was—partly, as he says, to be "liberated from the
tortures of boredom"—so, in a way, he reimagines bits and
pieces of Kafka for his own purposes. Kafka may have put
some funny ideas into his head, but that they serve different purposes is probably best exemplified by the fact that in
Schulz's book the character transformed into a cockroach
isn't the son but the father. Imagine Kafka imagining that.
Out of the question. Certain artistic predilections may be
similar, but these predilections are in league with wildly different desires. As you know, Schulz translated *The Trial* into
Polish in 1936. I wonder if Kafka was ever translated into
Yiddish.

Singer: Not that I know of. As a young man I read many
of the writers of the world in Yiddish; if Kafka would have
been translated into Yiddish, this would have been in the
thirties and I would have known about it. I'm afraid there is
no Yiddish translation. Or maybe there is and I don't know
about it, which is also possible.

Roth: Do you have any idea why Schulz wrote in Polish
rather than in Yiddish?

Singer: Most probably he was brought up in a home that
was already half assimilated. Probably his parents spoke
Polish. Many Jews in Poland—after Poland became independent, and even before—brought up their children to
speak Polish. That happened even in Russian Poland, but
especially in Galicia, the part of Poland that belonged to
Austria and where the Poles had a kind of autonomy and
were not culturally suppressed. It was a natural thing that
people who themselves spoke Polish brought up their children in this way. Whether it was good or bad I don't know.

But since Polish was, so to say, his mother tongue, Schulz had no choice, since a real writer will write not in a learned language but in the language he knows from his childhood. And Schulz's strength, of course, is in the language. I read him first in English, and though the translation is a good one, when I read him later in Polish I saw this strength very clearly.

Roth: Schulz was born of Jewish parents in Poland in 1892. You were born in 1904. Was it unusual for a Polish Jew of that generation to write in Polish, or to write in Yiddish, as you did?

Singer: The Jews had a number of important writers who wrote in Polish, and all of them were born more or less at this time, in the 1890s. Antoni Slonimski, Julian Tuwim, Józef Wittlin—all these writers were about this age. They were good writers, talented writers, but nothing special. Some of them, however, were very strong in the Polish language. Tuwim was a master of Polish. Slonimski was a grandson of Chaim Zelig Slonimski, who was the founder of the Hebrew newspaper *Hatsefira* in Warsaw. Slonimski was converted to Catholicism by his parents when he was a child, while Tuwim and Wittlin remained Jews, though Jews only in name. They had very little to do with Yiddish writers. My older brother, Israel Joshua Singer, was born more or less at the same time and was a known Yiddish writer in Poland and had no association with either of these writers. I was still a beginner, in Poland, and I certainly had nothing to do with them. We Yiddish writers looked at them as people who had left their roots and culture and become a part of Polish culture, which we considered younger and perhaps less important than our culture. They felt that we Yiddish writers were writing for ignorant people, poor people, people without education, while they were writing for readers who went to universities. So we both had a good reason to despise each other. Though the truth is, they had no choice and we had no choice. They didn't know Yiddish, we didn't know Polish. Although I was born in Poland, Polish was not as close to me as Yiddish. And I spoke it with an accent. As a matter of fact, I speak all languages with an accent.

Roth: Not Yiddish, I take it.

Singer: Yes. The Litvaks say I speak Yiddish with an accent.

Roth: I want to ask you about Warsaw in the thirties. Schulz studied architecture in Lwów as a young man, and then, as far as I know, he returned to the Galician town of Drohobycz, where for the rest of his life he taught drawing in the high school. He did not leave Drohobycz for any significant length of time until his middle or late thirties, when he came to Warsaw. What kind of cultural atmosphere would he have found in Warsaw then?

Singer: There are two things to remember about Schulz. First of all, he was a terribly modest person. The very fact that he stayed in this town, which was far away from the center of everything, shows that he was highly modest, and also kind of afraid. He felt like a yokel who's afraid to come to the big city and to meet people who are already famous. He was afraid, most probably, that they would make fun of him or they would ignore him. I think this man was a bundle of nerves. He suffered from all the inhibitions that a writer can suffer. When you look at his picture you see the face of a man who never made peace with life. Tell me, Mr. Roth, he was not married. Did he have some girlfriends?

Roth: If his drawings are any indication, I would think he had strange relations with women. A recurring subject in the drawings that I've seen is female dominance and male submission. There is an eerie, almost tawdry erotic suggestiveness to some of these pictures—small, supplicating men looking not unlike Schulz himself and remote, half-naked adolescent girls or statuesque, painted shopgirls. They remind me a little of the "trashy" erotic world of another Polish writer, Witold Gombrowicz. Like Kafka, who also never married, Schulz is said to have had long and intense correspondences with women and to have lived a good deal of his erotic life through the mails. Jerzy Ficowski, his biographer, who wrote the introduction to the Penguin edition, says that *The Street of Crocodiles* began as a series of letters to a close woman friend. They must have been some letters. According to Ficowski, it was this woman who urged Schulz—who was indeed a deeply inhibited person —to see these letters as a work of literature. But to return to Schulz and Warsaw—what was the cultural life like when he got there in the middle thirties? What was the dominant mood or ideology among writers and intellectuals?

Singer: I would say they had almost the same movement that we have today—kind of leftist. This was true of the Jewish writers who were writing in Polish. They were all leftist or considered leftists by the old Polish writers, who looked upon these Jewish writers, actually, as intruders.

Roth: Because they were writing in Polish?

Singer: Because they were writing in Polish. They might have said, "Why the hell don't they write in their own jargon, their own Yiddish—what do they want from us Poles?" Still, in the thirties, these Jewish writers became very important despite their adversaries. First, because they were quite good writers, though not great writers; second, because they were leftists, and that was the trend then; and third, because they were energetic, they published often in the magazine *Wiadomosci Literackie,* they wrote for the variety theater, and so on. Sometimes these Jewish writers wrote things that sounded anti-Semitic to the Jews. Of course I did not agree that it was anti-Semitism, because some critics said the same thing about me. Although I wrote in Yiddish, they said, "Why do you write about Jewish thieves and Jewish prostitutes?" and I said, "Shall I write about Spanish thieves and Spanish prostitutes? I write about the thieves and prostitutes that I know."

Roth: When you wrote in praise of Schulz back in 1963, you did have certain criticisms to make of him. You said, "If Schulz had identified himself more with his own people, he might not have expended so much energy on imitation, parody, and caricature." I wonder if you have any more to say about that.

Singer: I felt so when I wrote this and I think I feel so too now. There is great mockery in the writing both of Schulz and of Kafka, although in Kafka the mockery is more hidden. I think that Schulz had enough power to write real serious novels but instead often wrote a kind of parody. And I think basically he developed this style because he was not really at home, neither at home among the Poles nor at home among the Jews. It's a style that's somewhat characteristic also of Kafka, because Kafka also felt that he had no roots. He was a Jew who wrote in German and lived in Czechoslovakia, where the language was actually Czech. It is true that Kafka might have been more assimilated than Schulz—he didn't live in as Jewish a town as Drohobycz, which was full of Hasidim, and his father was maybe more of an assimilationist than Schulz's father, but the situation was basically the same, and as stylists the two writers were more or less of the same cut.

Roth: It's possible to think of Schulz's "rootlessness" another way: not as something that held him back from writing serious novels but as a condition upon which his particular talent and imagination thrived.

Singer: Yes, of course, that is true. If a genuine talent cannot be nourished directly from the soil, he will be nourished by something else. But from my point of view, I would rather have liked to have seen him as a Yiddish writer. He wouldn't have had all the time to be as negative and mocking as he was.

Roth: I wonder if it isn't negativism and mockery that drive Schulz so much as boredom and claustrophobia. Perhaps what sets him off on what he calls a "counteroffensive of fantasy" is that he is a man of enormous artistic gifts and imaginative riches living out his life as a high school teacher in a provincial town where his family are merchants. Also, he is his father's son, and his father, as he describes him, was, at least in his later years, a highly entertaining but terrifying madman, a grand "heresiarch," fascinated, Schulz says, "by doubtful and problematical forms." That last might be a good description of Schulz himself, who seems to me wholly conscious of just how close to madness, or heresy, his own agitated imagination could carry him. I don't think that with Schulz, any more than with Kafka, the greatest difficulty was an inability to be at home with this people or with that people, however much that may have added to his troubles. From the evidence of this book, it looks as though Schulz could barely identify himself with reality, let alone with the Jews. One is reminded of Kafka's remark on his communal affiliations:

"What have I in common with the Jews? I have hardly anything in common with myself and should stand very quietly in the corner, content that I can breathe." Schulz needn't have remained in Drohobycz if he found it all that stifling. People can pick up and go. He could have stayed in Warsaw once he finally got there. But perhaps the claustrophobic environment that didn't suit the needs of the man was just what gave life to his kind of art. *Fermentation* is a favorite word of his. It may only have been in Drohobycz that Schulz's imagination fermented.

Singer: I think also that in Warsaw he felt he ought to get back to Drohobycz because in Warsaw everybody said, "Who is Schulz?" Writers are not really ready to see a young man from the provinces and immediately to say, "You are our brother, you are our teacher"—they are not inclined to do so. Most probably they said, "Another nuisance with a manuscript." Also, he was a Jew. And these Jewish writers in Poland, who were really the rulers of the literary field, they were cautious about the fact that they were Jews.

Roth: Cautious in what way?

Singer: They were called Jews by their adversaries, by those who did not like them. This was always the eternal reproach. "What are you doing, Mr. Tuwim, with your Hebrew name, writing in Polish? Why don't you go back to the ghetto with Israel Joshua Singer and the others?" That is the way it was. So when there came another Jew who writes Polish, they felt not really comfortable about it. Because there came another problem child.

Roth: I take it that it was easier to assimilate into artistic or intellectual circles than into the bourgeois world of Warsaw.

Singer: I would say that it was more difficult. I will tell you why. A Jewish lawyer, if he didn't like to be called Levin or Katz, could call himself Levinski or Kacinski and people didn't bother him. But about a writer they were always cautious. They would say, "You have nothing to do with us." I think that some small similarity exists even in this country with the Jewish writers who write in English and are at home in English. No writer here would say to Saul Bellow or to you, "Why don't you write in Yiddish, why don't you go back to East Broadway?" Yet some small part of that still exists. I would think that there are some conservative writers here or critics who would say that people like you are not really American writers. However, here the Jewish writers are not really ashamed of being Jewish and they don't apologize all the time. There, in Poland, there was an atmosphere of apologizing. There they tried to show how Polish they were. And they tried of course to know Polish better than the Poles, in which they succeeded. But still the Poles said they have nothing to do with us . . . Let me make it clearer. Let's say if we would have now, here, a goy who would write in Yiddish, if this goy would be a failure, we would leave him in peace. But if he would be a great success, we would say, "What are you doing with Yiddish? Why don't you go back to the goyim, we don't need you."

Roth: A Polish Jew of your generation writing in Polish would have been as strange a creature as that?

Singer: Almost. And if there would be many such people, let's say there would be six goyim who would write in Yiddish, and there would come a seventh one . . .

Roth: Yes, it's clearer. You make it clearer.

Singer: I once was sitting in the subway with the Yiddish writer S, who had a beard, and at this time, forty years ago, very few people had beards. And he liked women, so he looked over and sitting across from him was a young woman, and he seemed to be highly interested. I sat on the side and I saw it—he didn't see me. Suddenly right near him came in another man also with a beard, and he began to look at the same woman. When S saw another one with a beard, he got up and left. He suddenly realized his own ridiculous situation. And this woman, as soon as this other man came in, she must have thought, What's going on here, already two beards?

Roth: You had no beard.

Singer: No, no. Do I need everything? A bald head *and* a beard?

Roth: You left Poland in the middle thirties, some years before the Nazi invasion. Schulz remained in Drohobycz and was killed there by the Nazis in 1942. Coming here to talk to you, I was thinking about how you, the Jewish writer from Eastern Europe most nourished by the Jewish world and most bound to it, left that world to come to America, while the other major Jewish writers of your generation—Jews far more assimilated, far more drawn toward the contemporary currents in the larger culture, writers like Schulz in Poland, and Isaac Babel in Russia, and, in Czechoslovakia, Jirí Weil, who wrote some of the most harrowing stories I've read about the Holocaust—were destroyed in one ghastly way or another, either by Nazism or Stalinism. May I ask who or what encouraged you to leave before the horrors began? After all, to be exiled from one's native country and language is something that nearly all writers would dread and probably be most reluctant to accomplish voluntarily. Why did you do it?

Singer: I had all the reasons to leave. First of all, I was very pessimistic. I saw that Hitler was already in power in 1935 and he was threatening Poland with invasion. Nazis like Göring came to Poland to hunt and to vacation. Second,

I worked for the Yiddish press, and the Yiddish press was going down all the time—it has been ever since it has existed. And my way of living became very frugal—I could barely exist. And the main thing was that my brother was here; he had come about two years before. So I had all the reasons to run to America.

Roth: And, leaving Poland, did you have fears about losing touch with your material?

Singer: Of course, and the fear became even stronger when I got to this country. I came here and I saw that everybody speaks English. I mean, there was a Hadassah meeting, and so I went and expected to hear Yiddish. But I came in and there was sitting about two hundred women and I heard one word: "delicious, delicious, delicious." I didn't know what it was, but it wasn't Yiddish. I don't know what they gave them there to eat, but two hundred women were sitting and saying, "Delicious." By the way, this was the first English world I learned. Poland looked far away then. When a person who is close to you dies, in the first few weeks after his death he is as far from you, as far as a near person can ever be; only with the years does he become nearer, and then you can almost live with this person. This is what happened to me. Poland, Jewish life in Poland, is nearer to me now than it was then.

Milan Kundera

[1980]

THIS INTERVIEW is condensed from two conversations I had with Milan Kundera after reading a translated manuscript of his *Book of Laughter and Forgetting*—one conversation while he was visiting London for the first time, the other when he was on his first visit to the United States. He took these trips from France; since 1975 he and his wife have been living there as émigrés, in Rennes, where he taught at the university, and now in Paris. During our conversations, Kundera spoke sporadically in French but mostly in Czech, and his wife, Vera, served as his translator and mine. A final Czech text was translated into English by Peter Kussi.

Roth: Do you think the destruction of the world is coming soon?

Kundera: That depends on what you mean by the word *soon*.

Roth: Tomorrow or the day after.

Kundera: The feeling that the world is rushing to ruin is an ancient one.

Roth: So then we have nothing to worry about.

Kundera: On the contrary. If a fear has been present in the human mind for ages, there must be something to it.

Roth: In any event, it seems to me that this concern is the background against which all the stories in your latest book take place, even those that are of a decidedly humorous nature.

Kundera: If someone had told me as a boy, "One day you will see your nation vanish from the world," I would have considered it nonsense, something I couldn't possibly imagine. A man knows he is mortal, but he takes it for granted that his nation possesses a kind of eternal life. But after the Russian invasion of 1968, every Czech was confronted with the thought that his nation could be quietly erased from Europe, just as over the past five decades forty million Ukrainians have been quietly vanishing from the world without the world paying any heed. Or Lithuanians. Do you know that in the seventeenth century Lithuania was a powerful European nation? Today the Russians keep Lithuanians on their reservation like a half-extinct tribe; they are sealed off from visitors to prevent knowledge about their existence from reaching the outside. I don't know what the future holds for my own nation. It is certain that the Russians will do everything they can to dissolve it gradually into their own civilization. Nobody knows whether they will succeed. But the possibility is there. And the sudden realization that such a possibility exists is enough to change one's whole sense of life. Nowadays I see even Europe as fragile, mortal.

Roth: And yet, are not the fates of Eastern Europe and Western Europe radically different matters?

Kundera: As a concept of cultural history, Eastern Europe is Russia, with its quite specific history anchored in the Byzantine world. Bohemia, Poland, Hungary, just like Austria, have never been part of Eastern Europe. From the very beginning they have taken part in the great adventure of Western civilization, with its Gothic, its Renaissance, its Reformation—a movement that has its cradle precisely in this region. It was there, in Central Europe, that modern culture found its greatest impulses: psychoanalysis, structuralism, dodecaphony, Bartók's music, Kafka's and Musil's new aesthetics of the novel. The postwar annexation of Central Europe (or at least its major part) by Russian civilization caused Western culture to lose its vital center of gravity. It is the most significant event in the history of the West in our century, and we cannot dismiss the possibility that the end of Central Europe marked the beginning of the end for Europe as a whole.

Roth: During the Prague Spring, your novel *The Joke* and your stories *Laughable Loves* were published in editions of 150,000. After the Russian invasion you were dismissed from your teaching post at the film academy and all your books were removed from the shelves of public libraries. Seven years later you and your wife tossed a few books and some clothes in the back of your car and drove off to France, where you've become one of the most widely read of foreign authors. How do you feel as an émigré?

Kundera: For a writer, the experience of living in a number of countries is an enormous boon. You can only understand the world if you see it from several sides. My latest book [*The Book of Laughter and Forgetting*], which came into being in France, unfolds in a special geographic space: those events that take place in Prague are seen through Western European eyes, while what happens in France is seen through the eyes of Prague. It is an encounter of two worlds. On one side, my native country: in the course of a mere half century, it experienced democracy, fascism, revolution, Stalinist terror as well as the disintegration of Stalinism, German and Russian occupation, mass deportations, the death of the West in its own land. It is thus sinking under the weight of history and looks at the world with immense skepticism. On the other side, France: for centuries it was the center of the world and nowadays it is suffering from the lack of great historic events. This is why it revels in radical ideological postures. It is the lyrical, neurotic expectation of some great deed of its own, which is not coming, however, and will never come.

Roth: Are you living in France as a stranger or do you feel culturally at home?

Kundera: I am enormously fond of French culture and I am greatly indebted to it. Especially to the older literature. Rabelais is dearest to me of all writers. And Diderot. I love his *Jacques le fataliste* as much as I do Laurence Sterne. Those were the greatest experimenters of all time in the form of the novel. And their experiments were, so to say, amusing, full of happiness and joy, which have by now vanished from French literature and without which everything in art loses its significance. Sterne and Diderot understood the novel as a great game. They discovered the humor of the novelistic form. When I hear learned arguments that the novel has exhausted its possibilities, I have precisely the opposite feeling: in the course of its history the novel missed many of its possibilities. For example, impulses for the development of the novel hidden in Sterne and Diderot have not been picked up by any successors.

Roth: *The Book of Laughter and Forgetting* is not called a novel, and yet in the text you declare: This book is a novel in the form of variations. So then, is it a novel or not?

Kundera: As far as my own quite personal aesthetic judgment goes, it really is a novel, but I have no wish to force this opinion on anyone. There is enormous freedom latent within the novelistic form. It is a mistake to regard a certain stereotyped structure as the inviolable essence of the novel.

Roth: Yet surely there is something that makes a novel a novel and that limits this freedom.

Kundera: A novel is a long piece of synthetic prose based on play with invented characters. These are the only limits. By the term *synthetic* I have in mind the novelist's desire to grasp his subject from all sides and in the fullest possible completeness. Ironic essay, novelistic narrative, autobiographical fragment, historical fact, flight of fantasy—the synthetic power of the novel is capable of combining everything into a unified whole like the voices of polyphonic music. The unity of a book need not stem from the plot but can be provided by the theme. In my latest book there are two such themes: laughter and forgetting.

Roth: Laughter has always been close to you. Your books provoke laughter through humor or irony. When your characters come to grief it is because they bump against a world that has lost its sense of humor.

Kundera: I learned the value of humor during the time of Stalinist terror. I was twenty then. I could always recognize a person who was not a Stalinist, a person whom I needn't fear, by the way he smiled. A sense of humor was a trustworthy sign of recognition. Ever since, I have been terrified by a world that is losing its sense of humor.

Roth: In *The Book of Laughter and Forgetting*, though, something else is involved. In a little parable you compare the laughter of angels with the laughter of the devil. The devil laughs because God's world seems senseless to him; the angels laugh with joy because everything in God's world has its meaning.

Kundera: Yes, man uses the same physiological manifestation—laughter—to express two different metaphysical attitudes. Someone's hat drops on the coffin in a freshly dug grave, the funeral loses its meaning and laughter is born. Two lovers race through the meadow, holding hands, laughing. Their laughter has nothing to do with jokes or humor; it is the serious laughter of angels expressing their joy of being. Both kinds of laughter belong among life's pleasures, but when it is carried to extremes it also denotes a dual apocalypse: the enthusiastic laughter of angel-fanatics, who are so convinced of their world's significance that they are ready to hang anyone not sharing their joy. And the other laughter, sounding from the opposite side, which proclaims that everything has become meaningless, that even funerals are ridiculous and group sex a mere comical pantomime. Human life is bounded by two chasms: fanaticism on one side, absolute skepticism on the other.

Roth: What you now call the laughter of angels is a new term for the "lyrical attitude to life" of your previous novels. In one of your books you characterize the era of Stalinist terror as the reign of the hangman and the poet.

Kundera: Totalitarianism is not only hell but also the dream of paradise—the age-old dream of a world where everybody lives in harmony, united by a single common will and faith, without secrets from one another. André Breton, too, dreamed of this paradise when he talked about the glass house in which he longed to live. If totalitarianism did not exploit these archetypes, which are deep inside us all and rooted deep in all religions, it could never attract so many people, especially during the early phases of its existence. Once the dream of paradise starts to turn into reality, however, here and there people begin to crop up who stand in its way, and so the rulers of paradise must build a little gulag on the side of Eden. In the course of time this gulag grows ever bigger and more perfect, while the adjoining paradise gets ever smaller and poorer.

Roth: In your book, the great French poet Éluard soars over paradise and gulag, singing. Is this bit of history that you mention in the book authentic?

Kundera: After the war, Paul Éluard abandoned surrealism and became the greatest exponent of what I might call the "poesy of totalitarianism." He sang for brotherhood, peace, justice, better tomorrows, he sang for comradeship and against isolation, for joy and against gloom, for innocence and against cynicism. When in 1950 the rulers of paradise sentenced Éluard's Prague friend, the surrealist Závis Kalandra, to death by hanging, Éluard suppressed his personal feelings of friendship for the sake of suprapersonal ideals and publicly declared his approval of his comrade's execution. The hangman killed while the poet sang.

And not just the poet. The whole period of Stalinist terror was a period of collective lyrical delirium. This has by now been completely forgotten, but it is the crux of the matter. People like to say: Revolution is beautiful; it is only the terror arising from it that is evil. But this is not true. The evil is already present in the beautiful, hell is already contained in the dream of paradise, and if we wish to understand the essence of hell we must examine the essence of the paradise from which it originated. It is extremely easy to condemn gulags, but to reject the totalitarian poesy that leads to the gulag by way of paradise is as difficult as ever. Nowadays, people all over the world unequivocally reject the idea of gulags, yet they are still willing to let themselves be hypnotized by totalitarian poesy and to march to new gulags to the tune of the same lyrical song piped by Éluard when he soared over Prague like the great archangel of the lyre, while the smoke of Kalandra's body rose to the sky from the crematory chimney.

Roth: What is so characteristic of your prose is the constant confrontation of the private and the public. But not in the sense that private stories take place against a political backdrop or that political events encroach on private lives. Rather, you continually show that political events are governed by the same laws as private happenings, so that your prose is a kind of psychoanalysis of politics.

Kundera: The metaphysics of man is the same in the private sphere as in the public one. Take the other theme of the book, forgetting. This is the great private problem of man: death as the loss of the self. But what is this self? It is the sum of everything we remember. Thus, what terrifies us about death is not the loss of the future but the loss of the past. Forgetting is a form of death ever present within life. This is the problem of my heroine, in desperately trying to preserve the vanishing memories of her beloved dead husband. But forgetting is also the great problem of politics. When a big power wants to deprive a small country of its national consciousness it uses the method of organized forgetting. This is what is currently happening in Bohemia. Contemporary Czech literature, insofar as it has any value at all, has not been printed for twelve years; 200 Czech writers have been proscribed, including the dead Franz Kafka; 145 Czech historians have been dismissed

97

from their posts, history has been rewritten, monuments have been demolished. A nation that loses awareness of its past gradually loses its self. And so the political situation has brutally illuminated the ordinary metaphysical problem of forgetting that we face all the time, every day, without paying any attention. Politics unmasks the metaphysics of private life, private life unmasks the metaphysics of politics.

Roth: In the sixth part of your book of variations the main heroine, Tamina, reaches an island where there are only children. In the end they hound her to death. Is this a dream, a fairy tale, an allegory?

Kundera: Nothing is more foreign to me than allegory, a story invented by the author in order to illustrate some thesis. Events, whether realistic or imaginary, must be significant in themselves, and the reader is meant to be naively seduced by their power and poetry. I have always been haunted by this image, and during one period of my life it kept recurring in my dreams: a person finds himself in a world of children, from which he cannot escape. And suddenly childhood, which we all lyricize and adore, reveals itself as pure horror. As a trap. This story is not allegory. But my book is a polyphony in which various stories mutually explain, illumine, complement one another. The basic event of the book is the story of totalitarianism, which deprives people of memory and thus retools them into a nation of children. All totalitarianisms do this. And perhaps our entire technical age does this, with its cult of the future, its cult of youth and childhood, its indifference to the past and mistrust of thought. In the midst of a relentlessly juvenile society, an adult equipped with memory and irony feels like Tamina on the isle of children.

Roth: Almost all your novels, in fact all the individual parts of your latest book, find their denouement in great scenes of coitus. Even that part which goes by the innocent name of "Mother" is but one long scene of three-way sex, with a prologue and epilogue. What does sex mean to you as a novelist?

Kundera: These days, when sexuality is no longer taboo, mere description, mere sexual confession, has become noticeably boring. How dated Lawrence seems, or even Henry Miller with his lyricism of obscenity! And yet certain erotic passages of Georges Bataille have made a lasting impression on me. Perhaps it is because they are not lyrical but philosophic. You are right that with me everything ends in great erotic scenes. I have the feeling that a scene of physical love generates an extremely sharp light that suddenly reveals the essence of characters and sums up their life situation. Hugo makes love to Tamina while she is desperately trying to think about lost vacations with her dead husband. The erotic scene is the focus where all the themes of the story converge and where its deepest secrets are located.

Roth: The last part, the seventh, actually deals with nothing but sexuality. Why does this part close the book rather than another, such as the much more dramatic sixth part, in which the heroine dies?

Kundera: Tamina dies, metaphorically speaking, amid the laughter of angels. Through the last section of the book, on the other hand, resounds the contrary kind of laugh, the kind heard when things lose their meaning. There is a certain imaginary dividing line beyond which things appear senseless and ridiculous. A person asks himself: Isn't it nonsensical for me to get up in the morning? to go to work? to strive for anything? to belong to a nation just because I was born that way? Man lives in close proximity to this boundary and can easily find himself on the other side. That boundary exists everywhere, in all areas of human life and even in the deepest, most biological of all: sexuality. And precisely because it is the deepest region of life, the question posed to sexuality is the deepest question. This is why my book of variations can end with no variation but this.

Roth: Is this, then, the furthest point you have reached in your pessimism?

Kundera: I am wary of the words *pessimism* and *optimism*. A novel does not assert anything; a novel searches and poses questions. I don't know whether my nation will perish and I don't know which of my characters is right. I invent stories, confront one with another, and by this means I ask questions. The stupidity of people comes from having an answer for everything. The wisdom of the novel comes from having a question for everything. When Don Quixote went out into the world, that world turned into a mystery before his eyes. That is the legacy of the first European novel to the entire subsequent history of the novel. The novelist teaches the reader to comprehend the world as a question. There is wisdom and tolerance in that attitude. In a world built on sacrosanct certainties the novel is dead. The totalitarian world, whether founded on Marx, Islam, or anything else, is a world of answers rather than questions. There the novel has no place. In any case, it seems to me that all over the world people nowadays prefer to judge rather than to understand, to answer rather than to ask, so that the voice of the novel can hardly be heard over the noisy foolishness of human certainties.

Edna O'Brien

T HE IRISH WRITER Edna O'Brien, who has lived in
London now for many years, moved recently to a
wide boulevard of imposing nineteenth-century fa-
çades, a street that in the 1870s, when it was built, was
renowned, she tells me, for its mistresses and kept women.
The real estate agents have taken to calling this corner of
the Maida Vale district "the Belgravia of tomorrow"; at the
moment it looks a little like a builder's yard because of all
the renovation going on.

O'Brien works in a quiet study that looks out to the green
lawn of an immense private garden at the rear of her flat, a
garden probably many times larger than the farm village in
County Clare where she attended mass as a child. There is
a desk, a piano, a sofa, a rosy Oriental carpet deeper in color
than the faint marbleized pink of the walls, and, through
the French doors that open onto the garden, enough plane
trees to fill a small park. On the mantel of the fireplace
there are photographs of the writer's two grown sons from
an early marriage—"I live here more or less alone"—and

the famous lyrical photograph of the profile of a very young Virginia Woolf, the heroine of O'Brien's *Virginia: A Play*. On the desk, which is set to look out toward the church steeple at the far end of the garden, there's a volume of J. M. Synge's collected works open to a chapter in *The Aran Islands;* a volume of Flaubert's correspondence lies on the sofa, the pages turned to an exchange with George Sand. While waiting for me to arrive, she has been signing pages of a special edition of fifteen thousand copies of her selected stories and listening to a record of rousing choruses from Verdi operas in order to help her get through.

Because everything she's wearing for the interview is black, you cannot miss the white skin, the green eyes, the auburn hair. The coloring is dramatically Irish—as is the mellifluous fluency.

Roth: In *Malone Dies*, your compatriot Samuel Beckett writes: "Let us say before I go any further, that I forgive nobody. I wish them all an atrocious life in the fires of icy hell and in the execrable generations to come." This quotation stands as the epigraph of *Mother Ireland*, a memoir you published in 1976. Did you mean to suggest by this epigraph that your own writing about Ireland isn't wholly uncontaminated by such sentiments? Frankly, I don't feel such harshness in your work.

O'Brien: I picked the epigraph because I am, or was, especially at that time, unforgiving about lots of things in my life, and I picked somebody who said it more eloquently and more ferociously than I could say it.

Roth: The fact is that your fiction argues *against* your unforgivingness.

O'Brien: To some extent it does, but that is because I am a creature of conflicts. When I vituperate, I subsequently feel I should appease. That happens throughout my life. I am not a natural out-and-out hater any more than I am a natural, or thorough, out-and-out lover, which means I am often rather at odds with myself and others!

Roth: Who is *the* unforgiven creature in your imagination?

O'Brien: Up to the time he died, which was a year ago, it was my father. But through death a metamorphosis happens: within. Since he died I have written a play about him embodying all his traits—his anger, his sexuality, his rapaciousness, et cetera—and now I feel differently toward him. I do not want to relive my life with him or be reincarnated as the same daughter, but I do forgive him. My mother is a different matter. I loved her, overloved her, yet she visited a different legacy on me, an all-embracing guilt. I still have a sense of her over my shoulder, judging.

Roth: Here you are, a woman of experience, talking about forgiving your mother and father. Do you think that still worrying those problems has largely to do with your being a writer? If you weren't a writer, if you were a lawyer, if you were a doctor, perhaps you wouldn't be thinking about these people so much.

O'Brien: Absolutely. It's the price of being a writer. One is dogged by the past—pain, sensations, rejections, all of it. I do believe that this clinging to the past is a zealous, albeit hopeless, desire to reinvent it so that one could change it. Doctors, lawyers, and many other stable citizens are not afflicted by a persistent memory. In their way, they might be just as disturbed as you or I, except that they don't know it. They don't delve.

Roth: But not all writers feast on their childhood as much as you have.

O'Brien: I am obsessive, also I am industrious. Besides, the time when you are most alive and most aware is in childhood, and one is trying to recapture that heightened awareness.

Roth: From the point of view not of a daughter or of a woman but of a fiction writer, do you consider yourself fortunate in your origins—having been born in the isolated reaches of Ireland, raised on a lonely farm in the shadow of a violent father, and educated by nuns behind the latched gate of a provincial convent? As a writer, how much or how little do you owe to the primitive rural world you often describe in stories about the Ireland of your childhood?

O'Brien: There's no telling, really. If I had grown up on the steppes of Russia or in Brooklyn—my parents lived there when they were first married—my material would have been different but my apprehension might be just the same. I happened to grow up in a country that was and is breathlessly beautiful, so the feeling for nature, for verdure, and for the soil was instilled into me. Secondly, there was no truck with culture or literature, so that my longing to write sprung up of its own accord, was spontaneous. The only books in our house were prayer books, cookery books, and blood-stock reports. I was privy to the world around me, was aware of everyone's little history, the stuff from which stories and novels are made. On the personal level, it was pretty drastic. So all these things combined to make me what I am.

Roth: But are you surprised that you survived the isolated farm and the violent father and the provincial convent without having lost the freedom of mind to be able to write?

O'Brien: I am surprised by my own sturdiness, yes, but I do not think that I am unscarred. Such things as driving a car or swimming are quite beyond me. In a lot of ways I feel a cripple. The body was as sacred as a tabernacle and every-thing a potential occasion of sin. It is funny now, but not that funny—the body contains the life story just as much as the brain. I console myself by thinking that if one part is destroyed another flourishes.

Roth: Was there enough money around when you were growing up?

O'Brien: No—but there had been! My father liked horses and liked leisure. He inherited a great deal of land and a beautiful stone house, but he was profligate and the land got given away or squandered in archetypal Irish fashion. Cousins who came home from America brought us clothes, and I inherited from my mother a certain childish pleasure in these things. Our greatest excitement was these visits, these gifts of trinkets and things, these signals of an out-side, cosmopolitan world, a world I longed to enter.

Roth: I'm struck, particularly in the stories of rural Ire-land during the war years, by the vastness and precision of your recall. You seem to remember the shape, texture, color, and dimensions of every object your eye may have landed upon while you were growing up—not to mention the human significance of all you saw, heard, smelled, tasted, and touched. The result is prose like a piece of fine mesh-work, a net of detail that enables you to contain all the long-ing and pain and remorse that surge through the fiction. What I want to ask is how you account for this ability to reconstruct with such passionate exactness an Irish world you haven't fully lived in for decades? How does your memory keep it alive, and why won't this vanished world leave you alone?

O'Brien: At certain times I am sucked back there, and the ordinary world and the present time recede. This recollection, or whatever it is, invades me. It is not something that I can summon up; it simply comes and I am the servant of it. My hand does the work and I don't have to think; in fact, were I to think, it would stop the flow. It's like a dam in the brain that bursts.

Roth: Do you visit Ireland to help along the recall?

O'Brien: When I visit Ireland, I always secretly hope that something will spark off the hidden world and the hidden stories waiting to be released, but it doesn't happen like that! It happens, as you well know, much more convolutedly, through one's dreams, through chance, and, in my case, through the welter of emotion stimulated by a love affair and its aftermath.

Roth: I wonder if you haven't chosen the way you live—living by yourself—to prevent anything emotionally too powerful from separating you from that past.

O'Brien: I'm sure I have. I rail against my loneliness but it is as dear to me as the thought of unity with a man. I have often said that I would like to divide my life into alternating periods of penance, cavorting, and work, but as you can see that would not strictly fit in with a conventional married life.

Roth: Most American writers I know would be greatly unnerved by the prospect of living away from the country that's their subject and the source of their language and obsessions. Many Eastern European writers I know remain behind the Iron Curtain because the hardships of totalitarianism seem preferable to the dangers, for a writer, of exile. If ever there was a case for a writer's staying within earshot of the old neighborhood, it's been provided by two Americans who, to my mind, together constitute the spine of my country's literature in the twentieth century: Faulkner, who settled back in Mississippi after a brief period abroad, and Bellow, who, after his wanderings, returned to live and teach in Chicago. Now, we all know that neither Beckett nor Joyce seemed to want or to need a base in Ireland once they began experimenting with their Irish endowment, but do *you* ever feel that leaving Ireland as a very young woman and coming to London to make a life has cost you anything as a writer? Isn't there an Ireland other than the Ireland of your youth that might have been turned to your purposes?

O'Brien: To establish oneself in a particular place and to use it as the locale for fiction is both a strength to the writer and a signpost to the reader. But you have to go if you find your roots too threatening, too impinging. Joyce said that Ireland is the sow that eats its farrow. He was referring to its attitude toward its writers—it savages them. It is no accident that our two greatest illustrissimi, himself and Mr. Beckett, left and stayed away, though they never lost their particular Irish consciousness. In my own case, I do not think that I would have written anything if I had stayed. I feel I would have been watched, would have been judged (even more!), and would have lost that priceless commodity called freedom. Writers are always on the run, and I was on the run from many things. Yes, I dispossessed myself and I am sure that I lost something, lost the continuity, lost the day-to-day contact with reality. However, compared with Eastern European writers, I have the advantage that I can always go back. For them it must be terrible, the finality of it, the utter banishment, like a soul shut out of heaven.

Roth: Will you go back?

O'Brien: Intermittently. Ireland is very different now, a much more secular land, where, ironically, both the love of literature and the repudiation of literature are on the wane.

Ireland is becoming as materialistic and as callow as the rest of the world. Yeats's line—"Romantic Ireland's dead and gone"—has indeed come to fruition.

Roth: In my foreword to your book *A Fanatic Heart*, I quote what Frank Tuohy, in an essay about James Joyce, had to say about the two of you: that while Joyce, in *Dubliners* and *A Portrait of the Artist as a Young Man*, was the first Irish Catholic to make his experience and surroundings recognizable, "the world of Nora Barnacle [the former chambermaid who became Joyce's wife] had to wait for the fiction of Edna O'Brien." Can you tell me how important Joyce has been to you? A story of yours like "Tough Men," about the bamboozling of a scheming shopkeeper by an itinerant con man, seems to me right out of some rural *Dubliners*, and yet you don't seem to have been challenged by Joyce's linguistic and mythic preoccupations. What has he meant to you, what if anything have you taken or learned from him, and how intimidating is it for an Irish writer to have as precursor this great verbal behemoth who has chewed up everything Irish in sight?

O'Brien: In the constellation of geniuses, he is a blinding light and father of us all. (I exclude Shakespeare because for Shakespeare no human epithet is enough.) When I first read Joyce, it was a little book edited by T. S. Eliot that I bought on the quays in Dublin, secondhand, for fourpence. Before that, I had read very few books and they were mostly gushing and outlandish. I was a pharmaceutical apprentice who dreamed of writing. Now here was "The Dead" and a section of *A Portrait of the Artist as a Young Man*, which stunned me not only by the bewitchment of style but because they were so true to life, they *were* life. Then, or rather later, I came to read *Ulysses*, but as a young girl I balked, because it was really too much for me, it was too inaccessible and too masculine, apart from the famous Molly Bloom section. I now think *Ulysses* is the most diverting, brilliant, intricate, and unboring book that I have ever read. I can pick it up at any time, read a few pages, and feel that I have just had a brain transfusion. As for his being intimidating, it doesn't arise—he is simply out of bounds, beyond us all, "the far Azores," as he might call it.

Roth: Let's go back to the world of Nora Barnacle, to how the world looks to the Nora Barnacles, those who remain in Ireland and those who take flight. At the center of virtually all your stories is a woman, generally a woman on her own, battling isolation and loneliness, or seeking love, or recoiling from the surprises of adventuring among men. You write about women without a taint of ideology or, as far as I can see, any concern with taking a correct position.

O'Brien: The correct position is to write the truth, to write what one feels regardless of any public consideration or any clique. I think an artist never takes a position either through expedience or umbrage. Artists detest and suspect positions because you know that the minute you take a fixed position you are something else—you are a journalist or you are a politician. What I am after is a bit of magic, and I do not want to write tracts or to read them. I have depicted women in lonely, desperate, and often humiliated situations, very often the butt of men and almost always searching for an emotional catharsis that does not come. This is my territory and one that I know from hard-earned experience. If you want to know what I regard as the principal crux of female despair, it is this: in the Greek myth of Oedipus and in Freud's exploration of it, the son's desire for his mother is admitted; the infant daughter also desires her mother but it is unthinkable, either in myth, in fantasy, or in fact, that that desire can be consummated.

Roth: Yet you can't be oblivious to the changes in "consciousness" that have been said to be occasioned by the women's movement.

O'Brien: Yes, certain things have been changed for the better—women are not chattel, they express their right to earn as much as men, to be respected, not to be "the second sex"—but in the mating area things have not changed. Attraction and sexual love are spurred not by consciousness but by instinct and passion, and in this men and women are radically different. The man still has the greater authority and the greater autonomy. It's biological. The woman's fate is to receive the sperm and to retain it, but the man's is to give it and in the giving he spends himself and then subsequently withdraws. While she is in a sense being fed, he is in the opposite sense being drained, and to resuscitate himself he takes temporary flight. As a result, you get the woman's resentment at being abandoned, however briefly; his guilt at going; and, above all, his innate sense of self-protection in order to refind himself so as to reaffirm himself. Closeness is therefore always only relative. A man may help with the dishes and so forth, but his commitment is more ambiguous and he has a roving eye.

Roth: Are there no women as promiscuous?

O'Brien: They sometimes are but it doesn't give them the same sense of achievement. A woman, I dare to say, is capable of a deeper and more lasting love. I would also add that a woman is more afraid of being left. That still stands. Go into any women's canteen, dress department, hairdresser's, gymnasium, and you will see plenty of desperation and plenty of competition. People utter a lot of slogans but they are only slogans and what we feel and do is what determines us. Women are no more secure in their emotions than they ever were. They simply are better at coming to terms with them. The only real security would be to turn away from men, to detach, but that would be a little death—at least for me it would.

Roth: Why do you write so many love stories? Is it because of the importance of the subject or because, like many others in our profession, once you grew up and left home and chose the solitary life of a writer, sexual love inevitably became the strongest sphere of experience to which you continued to have access?

O'Brien: First of all, I think love replaced religion for me in my sense of fervor. When I began to look for earthly love (i.e., sex), I felt that I was cutting myself off from God. By taking on the mantle of religion, sex assumed proportions that are rather far-fetched. It became the central thing in my life, the goal. I was very prone to the Heathcliff/Mr. Rochester syndrome and still am. The sexual excitement was to a great extent linked with pain and separation. My sexual life is pivotal to me, as I believe it is for everyone else. It takes up a lot of time both in the thinking and in the doing, the former often taking pride of place. For me, primarily, it is secretive and contains elements of mystery and plunder. My daily life and my sexual life are not of a whole—they are separated. Part of my Irish heritage!

Roth: What's most difficult about being both a woman and a writer? Are there difficulties you have writing as a woman that I don't have as a man? And do you imagine that there might be difficulties I have that you don't?

O'Brien: I think it is different being a man and being a woman—it is very different. I think you as a man have waiting for you in the wings of the world a whole cortege of women—potential wives, mistresses, muses, nurses. Women writers do not have that bonus. The examples are numerous: the Brontë sisters, Jane Austen, Carson Mc-Cullers, Flannery O'Connor, Emily Dickinson, Marina Tsvetayeva. I think it was Dashiell Hammett who said he wouldn't want to live with a woman who had more problems than he had. I think the signals men get from me alarm them.

Roth: You will have to find a Leonard Woolf.

O'Brien: I do not want a Leonard Woolf. I want Lord Byron and Leonard Woolf mixed in together.

Roth: But does the job fundamentally come down to the same difficulties then, regardless of gender?

O'Brien: Absolutely. There is no difference at all. You, like me, are trying to make something out of nothing and the anxiety is extreme. Flaubert's description of his room echoing with curses and cries of distress could be any writer's room. Yet I doubt that we would welcome an alternative life. There is something stoical about soldiering on all alone.

An Exchange with
Mary McCarthy

141 rue de Rennes
75006 Paris
January 11, 1987

Dear Philip:

Thank you for sending me your book [*The Counterlife*], which I started reading with excitement and enthusiasm that continued to mount through the section in Israel and the El Al part, too, but that left me in England at Christmastime, not to return, and I don't know why exactly. Perhaps you have a better guess than I. It is probably never wise to give an author a negative or "qualified" opinion of his book, but I am moved to do so because I liked your last book, all the parts of it, very, very much and I guess because I assumed that if you sent me your book it was because you were interested in my opinion of it.

So I will try to say what I think. The high point, for me, was the Hebron chapter, brilliant in every way and laying the whole problem—Israel—out with honesty and clarity. As I read, I kept contrasting it with an imaginary novel by

Bellow. I also liked the earlier, dentist's office parts, the bi-furcation of the Zuckerman figure, and the independent existence, like an angleworm's, achieved by the separate pieces. It seems to me a pity that this idea (unless I failed to understand) seems to have been lost sight of in *Gloucester-shire* and *Christendom*, which, on their own, wearied me. With what feels to me like pathology—a severe case of anti-anti-semitism.

I remember Philip Rahv saying that all Gentiles, without exception, were anti-semitic. If so, that is an awful problem for a Jewish novelist who wants to have Gentile charac-ters in his work. Maybe the English sections of *The Coun-terlife* won't offend Jewish readers, but they irritated and offended. I'm not a Christian (I don't believe in God), but to the extent that I am and can't help being (just as a "nice Jewish boy" can't help being Jewish), I bridle at your picture of Christianity. There's more to Christmas, that is, to the idea of the Incarnation, than Jew-hatred. True, I've some-times thought that all our Christmas-caroling must be offensive to non-sharers in the bliss of that wondrous occa-sion. But perhaps non-sharers, those outside the Law, can get the general idea or try to, as I hope I would try to get the idea of the Wailing Wall, repellent as it is to me, if I were taken to it. And I confess that the crib with angels and ani-mals and a star is to me a more sympathetic idea than the Wailing Wall; as a non-believer, I greatly prefer it. The re-sidual Christian in me probably looks forward happily to the millennium and the conversion of the Jews, including Philip Roth. Philip Rahv too.

Then all that circumcision business. Why so excited about making a child a Jew by taking a knife to him? I have nothing against circumcision; the men of my generation were all circumcised—a de rigueur pediatric procedure—and my son's generation, too. It must have been Freudian influences somehow that in the Forties persuaded educated people that circumcision was a superstition (I even heard it called a dirty Jewish superstition) which robbed the male of full sexual enjoyment in the pretended interest of hygiene. So then it became unchic to have a baby boy circumcised. Religion did not enter into any of this, any more than it did into the breast-feeding, anti-breast-feeding discussion. And if Nathan Zuckerman *isn't* a believing Jew, why is he so hung up on this issue?

Forgive me if all this is disagreeable to you. It is strange to *me* that *The Counterlife* should remind me so forcibly that I am a Christian whatever I choose to imagine. The last time in my adult life that I felt anything like that was in Hanoi in 1968 with U.S. bombers overhead when I reacted, in the privacy of my thoughts, against the Marxist-Buddhist orthodoxy that I felt in the local leaders.

I am sorry that we never got together with Leon [Botstein] this past fall. Next year, I hope. I last saw him at a Christmas-carol singing, just before we flew back here.

Happy New Year, sincerely,
Mary

15 Fawcett St.
London SW10
January 17, 1987

Dear Mary:

Thanks for writing at such length about the book. Of course I would want to know what you thought and that is indeed why I sent you the book, and I'm delighted that you have been so candid with me.

To begin with, it sounds as though you were held by an awful lot of it, virtually everything up to the last two chapters. I won't go into a discussion of why the structural idea was not abandoned in the last two chapters but in fact sealed and reinforced, since I think that would take too long and probably sound like a lecture, which I don't intend to deliver to you, of all people.

I happen to be known (to Jews) for having "a severe case of anti-anti-Semitism," as you claim to have yourself, *as does Zuckerman*. I think here all these issues seem to have struck you *outside* the narrative context and the thematic preoccupations of the book.

Let me take up your points one at a time.

1. Rahv's statement that all Gentiles are anti-Semitic. This is, of course, exactly what Zuckerman hears at Agor [a Jewish settlement on Israel's West Bank]. He is hardly sympathetic to that assertion. How could he have married Maria Freshfield if he were? Though that's the least of it: it simply runs counter to his experience, period. The irony, it seemed to me, was that, having been exposed to a kind of rhetoric he finds profoundly unpersuasive, he then comes back to London and runs smack into Maria's sister, her hymn of [anti-Semitic] hate, and her insinuations about [the anti-Semitism of] Maria's mother. There is then the [anti-Semitic] incident at the restaurant and the conversation with Maria [about English anti-Semitism] that gets so hopelessly out of hand. None of this is evidence that all Gentiles are anti-Semitic. But it does force Zuckerman—the very same fellow so skeptical, to put it mildly, of Lippman's [Agor] manifesto—to have to deal with a phenomenon previously unknown to him, though hardly unknown in the world (or in England, for that matter). I wanted him aston-

ished, caught off-balance, *educated*. I wanted him threatened with the loss of this woman he adores because of this stinking, hideous old problem that seems to have turned up right at the heart of the family into which he has married. Truly, I don't see what there is to be offended by there, and maybe it wasn't this that offended and irritated you.

2. "There's more to Christmas, that is, to the idea of the Incarnation, than Jew-hatred." But Zuckerman doesn't say there isn't. He does, however, articulate (for the first time anywhere in fiction, as far as I know) how many a Jew happens to feel when confronted with this stuff. Whether justified or not, he is mildly affronted, and what he says is not quite what you suggest he says. "But between me and *church devotion* [*not* the Incarnation] there is an unbridgeable world of feeling, a natural and thoroughgoing incompatibility—I have the emotions of a spy in the adversary's camp and feel I'm overseeing the very rites that *embody the ideology* that's been responsible for the persecution and mistreatment of Jews . . . I just find the religion . . . profoundly inappropriate, and never more so than when the congregants are observing the highest standards of liturgical decorum and the clerics most beautifully enunciating the doctrine of love." (I've added the italics.) Now, you may not think such reasoning is sound, but that even an intelligent Jew is capable of reasoning in just that way is a fact. I was trying to be truthful.

3. ". . . as a non-believer, I greatly prefer it," you say, meaning "the crib with angels and animals and a star" to "the Wailing Wall." That is again where you and Zuckerman part company. As a non-believer, he prefers neither. He finds little to recommend the sanctification of either set of icons or symbols or whatever they all are taken together.

Furthermore, Zuckerman behaves beautifully at the carol service and therefore *looks* at least as you might look at the Wailing Wall, where you say you would try to get the idea, repellent as it is to you. I think you have—a word I hate—overreacted to these few observations, which he himself knows are determined by his Jewishness and nothing more. "Yet, Jewishly, I still thought, what *do* they need all this stuff for?" His objections really are aesthetic, aren't they? "Though frankly I've always felt that the place where Christianity gets dangerously, vulgarly obsessed with the miraculous is Easter, the Nativity has always struck me as a close second to the Resurrection in nakedly addressing the most childish need." You say you bridle at my picture of Christianity, and if you bridle at this, so be it. But you do see it has nothing to do, or not much to do, with "Jew-hatred."

Now to speak only as a novelist (which I am far more than I am a Jew). If Zuckerman hadn't gone to [Agor in] Judea and heard what he heard there I would never have had this scene in the church or have had him think these thoughts. But it seemed to me only fair that—no, I don't mean that: it seemed to me simply that the one scene called forth the other. I didn't want all his skepticism focused on Jewish ritual and none of it on Christian. That would have had all the wrong implications and made him see what he is not, and that is a self-hating Jew who—to borrow a phrase—casts a cold eye only on his own.

4. "Why so excited about making a child a Jew by taking a knife to him?" Context, context, context. This is his response, his aggressive and angry response, to the suggestion that his child will have to be christened in order to please Maria's mother. The paean to circumcision arises out of that threat. If you won't listen to me on this subject,

listen to Maria. In her letter (written in fact by Z., but that subject I'm not going into) she writes, "If it's this that establishes for you the truth of your paternity—that regains for you the truth of your *own* paternity—so be it." Here I was thinking thoughts that the reader can hardly be expected to follow. I was thinking about Zuckerman and his own father, and the word *bastard* that the old man Zuckerman [in *Zuckerman Unbound*] whispers to Nathan from his deathbed. The circumcision of little English-American Z. is big American Z. settling that issue at last. That is my business, I suppose, but it figured in the thing.

I think you also fail to see how serious this circumcision business is to Jews. I am still hypnotized by uncircumcised men when I see them at my swimming pool locker room [in London]. The damn thing never goes unregistered. Most Jewish men I know have similar reactions, and when I was writing the book, I asked several of my equally secular Jewish male friends if they could have an uncircumcised son, and they all said no, sometimes without having to think about it and sometimes after the nice long pause that any rationalist takes before opting for the irrational. Why is N.Z. hung up on circumcision? I hope that's clearer now.

5. "Forgive me if all this is disagreeable to you." I would have had to forgive you if you had been "agreeable."

Yours,
Philip

Pictures of Malamud

"Mourning is a hard business," Cesare said. "If people knew, there'd be less death."

—From Malamud's "Life Is Better Than Death"

[1986]

In FEBRUARY 1961 I traveled west from Iowa City, where I was teaching in the Writers' Workshop of the university and finishing a second book, to give a lecture at a small community college in Monmouth, Oregon. A buddy from my graduate school days was teaching there and had arranged the invitation. I accepted not only because of the opportunity the trip afforded me to see, for the first time in five years, my friends the Bakers, but because Bob Baker promised that if I came he'd arrange for me to meet Bernard Malamud.

Bern taught nearby at the state university in Corvallis. He'd been in Corvallis, Oregon (pop. 15,000), since leaving New York (pop. 8,000,000) and a night-school teaching job there in 1949—twelve years in the Far West instructing freshmen in the fundamentals of English composition and writing the unorthodox baseball novel *The Natural;* his masterpiece set in darkest Brooklyn, *The Assistant;* as well as four or five of the best American short stories I'd ever read (or I ever will). The other stories weren't bad either.

In the early fifties I was reading Malamud's stories, later collected in *The Magic Barrel,* as they appeared—the day they appeared—in *Partisan Review* and the old *Commentary.* He seemed to me to be doing no less for his lonely Jews and their peculiarly immigrant, Jewish forms of failure— for those Malamudians "who never stopped hurting"—than was Samuel Beckett, in his longer fiction, for misery-ridden Molloy and Malone. Both writers, while bound imaginatively (though not communally) to the common life of the clan, severed racial memories from the larger social and historical setting and then, focusing as narrowly as they could on the dismal daily round of resistance borne by the most helpless of their landsmen, created parables of frustration steeped in the gravity of the grimmest philosophers.

Not unlike Beckett, Malamud wrote of a meager world of pain in a language all his own, an English that appeared, even apart from the idiosyncratic dialogue, to have been pulled out of what one might have thought would be the most unmagical barrel around—the locutions, inversions, and diction of Jewish immigrant speech, a heap of broken verbal bones that looked, until he came along and made them dance to his sad tune, to be of use no longer to anyone other than a Borscht Belt comic or a professional nostalgist. Even when he pushed his parable prose to its limits, Malamud's metaphors retained a proverbial ring. At his most consciously original, when he sensed in his grimly told, impassioned tales the moment to sound his deepest note, he remained fixed to what seemed old and homely, emitting the most unadorned poetry to make matters even sadder than they already were: "He tried to say some sweet thing but his tongue hung in his mouth like dead fruit on a tree, and his heart was a black-painted window."

The forty-six-year-old man whom I met at the Bakers' little house in Monmouth, Oregon, in 1961 never let on that he could have written that or any such line. At first glance Bern looked to someone who'd grown up among such people like nothing so much as an insurance agent—he could have passed for one of my father's colleagues at the district office of Metropolitan Life. When Malamud entered the Bakers' hallway after having attended my lecture, when he stood there on the welcome mat removing his wet over-shoes, I saw a conscientious, courteous workingman of the kind whose kibitzing and conversation had been the back-ground music of my childhood, a stubborn, seasoned life insurance salesman who does not flee the snarling dog or alarm the children when he appears after dark at the top of the tenement stairwell. He doesn't frighten anyone but he doesn't make the place light up with laughter either: he is, after all, the insurance man, whom you can only beat by dying.

That was the other surprise about Malamud. So little laughter. No display at all of the playfulness that flickered on and off in those underheated, poorly furnished flats wherein were enacted the needs of his entombed. No sign from him of the eerie clowning that distinguishes *The Nat-ural*. There were Malamud stories like "Angel Levine"—and later "The Jewbird" and "Talking Horse"—where the joke seemed only an inch away from the art, where the charm of the art was how it humorously hovered at the edge of the joke, and yet, over twenty-five years, I remember him telling me two jokes. Jewish dialect jokes, expertly recounted, but that was it. For twenty-five years two jokes were enough.

There was no need to overdo anything other than the responsibility to his art. Bern didn't exhibit himself and didn't consider it necessary to exhibit his themes, certainly not casually to a stranger. He couldn't have exhibited himself had he even been foolish enough to try, and never being foolish was a small part of his larger burden. S. Levin, the Chaplinesque professor of *A New Life*, teaching his first college class with a wide-open fly, is hilariously foolish time and again, but not Bern. No more could Kafka have become a cockroach than could Malamud have metamorphosed into a Levin, comically outfoxed by an erotic mishap on the dark back roads of mountainous Oregon and sneaking homeward, half naked, at 3 A.M., beside him a sexually disgruntled barroom waitress dressed in only one shoe and a bra. Seymour Levin the ex-drunkard and Gregor Samsa the bug embody acts of colossal self-travesty, affording both authors a weirdly exhilarating sort of masochistic relief from the weight of sobriety and dignified inhibition that formed the cornerstone of their staid comportment. With Malamud, exuberant showmanship, like searing self-mockery, was to be revealed through what Heine called *Maskenfreiheit*, the freedom conferred by masks.

The sorrowing chronicler of need clashing with need, of need mercilessly resisted and abated only glancingly if at all, of blockaded lives racked with a need for the light, the lift, of a little hope—"A child throwing a ball straight up saw a bit of pale sky"—preferred to present himself as someone whose own need was nobody else's business. Yet his was a need so harsh that it makes one ache to imagine it. It was the need to consider long and seriously every last demand of a conscience torturously exacerbated by the pathos of need unabated. That was a theme of his that he couldn't hide entirely from anyone who thought at all about where the man who could have passed himself off as your insurance agent was joined to the parabolical moralist of the claustrophobic stories about "things you can't get past." In *The Assistant,* the petty criminal and drifter Frank Alpine, while doing penance behind the counter of a failing grocery store that he'd once helped to rob, has a "terrifying insight" about himself: "that all the while he was acting like he wasn't, he was a man of stern morality." I wonder if early in adult life Bern didn't have an insight about himself still more terrifying: that he was a man of stern morality who could act *only* like what he was.

Between our first meeting in Oregon in February 1961 and our last meeting in the summer of 1985 at his home in Bennington, Vermont, I rarely saw him more than a couple times a year, and for several years, after I'd published an essay about American Jewish writers in the *New York Review of Books* that examined *Pictures of Fidelman* and *The Fixer* from a perspective he didn't like—and couldn't have been expected to—we didn't see each other at all. In the mid-sixties, when I was a guest for long periods at the Yaddo artists' colony in Saratoga Springs, New York, a short drive from Bennington, he and his wife, Ann, would have me over when I felt like escaping for a few hours from the Yaddo solitude. In the seventies, when we were both members of the Yaddo corporation board, we'd see each other at the biannual meetings. When the Malamuds began to take refuge in Manhattan from the Vermont winters and I was still living in New York, we'd meet occasionally near their Gramercy Park apartment for dinner. And when Bern and Ann visited London, where I'd begun spending my time, they'd come to have dinner with Claire Bloom and me.

Though Bern and I ended up most evenings talking together about books and writing, we hardly ever alluded to each other's fiction and never seriously discussed it, observing an unwritten rule of propriety that exists among novelists, as among rival teammates in sports, who understand just how little candor can be sustained however deep the respect may run. Blake says, "Opposition is true friendship," and though that sounds admirably bracing, particularly to the argumentative, and subscribing to its wisdom probably works out well in the best of all possible worlds, among the writers in this world, where touchiness and pride can make for a potent explosive, one learns to settle for something a bit more amicable than outright opposition if one wants to have any true writer friends at all. Even those writers who adore opposition usually get about as much as they can stand from their daily work.

It was in London that we arranged to meet again after my 1974 *New York Review* essay and the exchange of letters about it that was to be the last communication between us for a couple of years. His letter had been characteristically terse and colloquial, a single sentence, sounding perhaps a little less fractious than it looked alone on that white sheet of typing paper inscribed above the tiny, measured signature. What I'd written about *Fidelman* and *The Fixer,* he informed me, "is your problem, not mine." I wrote right back to tell him that I'd probably done him a favor of precisely the kind William Blake advocated. I didn't have quite the gall to mention Blake, but that was more or less my tack: what I'd written would help him out. Not too awful as these exchanges go, but not one to ennoble either of us in the canon of literary correspondence.

The London reconciliation didn't take long for Bern and me to pull off. At 7:30 P.M. the doorbell rang and there, on the dot as always, were the Malamuds. Under the porch light I gave Ann a kiss and then, with my hand extended, plunged past her, advancing upon Bern, who with his own outstretched hand was briskly coming up the steps toward me. In our eagerness each to be the first to forgive—or perhaps to be forgiven—we wound up overshooting the handshake and kissing on the lips, rather like the poor baker Lieb and the even less fortunate Kobotsky at the conclusion of "The Loan." The two Jews in that Malamud tale, once immigrants together out of steerage, meet after many years of broken friendship and, at the back of Lieb's shop, listen to the stories of the afflictions in each other's lives, stories so affecting that Lieb forgets all about the bread in his oven, which goes up in smoke. "The loaves in the trays," the story ends, "were blackened bricks—charred corpses. Kobotsky and the baker embraced and sighed over their lost youth. They pressed mouths together and parted forever." We, on the other hand, remained friends for good.

In July 1985, just back from England, Claire and I drove north from Connecticut to have lunch and spend the afternoon with the Malamuds in Bennington. The summer before, they had made the two-and-a-half-hour trip down to us and then spent the night, but Bern wasn't equal to the journey now. The debilitating aftereffects of a stroke three years earlier were sapping his strength, and the effort not to submit without a fight to all the disabling physical problems had begun to beat even him down. I saw how weak he'd got as soon as we drove up. Bern, who always managed, regardless of the weather, to be waiting in the driveway to greet you and see you off, was out there all right in his poplin jacket, but as he nodded a rather grim welcome, he looked to be listing slightly to one side at the same time that he seemed to be holding himself, by dint of willpower alone, absolutely still, as though the least movement would send him crashing to the ground. The forty-six-year-old transplanted Brooklynite whom I'd met in the Far West, that undiscourageable round-the-clock worker with the serious, attentive face and the balding crown and the pitiless Corvallis haircut, whose serviceable surface mildness could have misled anyone about the molten obstinacy at the core —and probably was intended to—was now a frail and very sick old man, his tenacity about used up.

It was bypass surgery and the stroke and the medication that had done the job, but to a longtime reader of the man and his fiction it couldn't help but appear as if the pursuit of that unremitting aspiration that he shared with so many of his characters—to break through the iron limits of self and circumstance in order to live a better life—had finally taken its toll. Though he'd never said much to me about his childhood, from the little I knew about his mother's death when he was still a boy, about the father's poverty and the handicapped brother, I imagined that he'd had no choice but to forgo youth and accept adulthood at an early age. And now he looked it—like a man who'd had to be a man for just too long a time. I thought of his story "Take Pity," the most excruciating parable he ever wrote about life's unyieldingness even to—especially to—the most unyielding longings. When quizzed by Davidov, a heavenly census taker, about how a poor Jewish refugee died, Rosen, himself newly arrived among the dead, replies: "Broke in him something. That's how." "Broke what?" "Broke what breaks."

It was a sad afternoon. We tried talking in the living room before lunch, but concentration was a struggle for him, and though his was a will powerless to back away from any difficult task, it was disheartening to realize how imposing a challenge merely pursuing a friendly conversation had become.

As we were leaving the living room to have lunch outdoors on the back porch, Bern asked if he might read aloud to me later the opening chapters of a first draft of a novel. He'd never before asked my opinion of a work in progress, and I was surprised by the request. I was also perturbed and wondered throughout lunch what sort of book it could be, conceived and begun in the midst of all this hardship by a writer whose memory of even the multiplication tables had been clouded now for several years and whose vision, also impaired by the stroke, made shaving every morning what he'd wryly described to me as "an adventure."

After coffee Bern went to his study for the manuscript, a thin sheaf of pages meticulously typed and clipped together. Ann, whose back was bothering her, excused herself to take a rest, and when Bern settled himself again at the table it was to begin to read in his quiet, insistent way to Claire and me.

I noticed that around his chair, on the porch floor, were scattered crumbs from lunch. A tremor had made eating an adventure too, and yet he had driven himself to write these pages, to undertake once again the writer's ordeal. I remembered the opening of *The Assistant*, the picture of the aging grocer, Morris Bober, dragging the heavy milk cases in from the curb at six o'clock on a November morning; I remembered the exertion that kills him—already close to physical collapse, Bober nonetheless goes out at night to clear six inches of fresh March snow from the sidewalk in front of the imprisoning store. When I got home that evening, I reread the pages describing the grocer's last great effort to do his job.

> To his surprise the wind wrapped him in an icy jacket, his apron flapping noisily. He had expected, the last of March, a milder night . . . He flung another load of snow into the street. "A better life," he muttered.

It turned out that not many words were typed on each page and that the chapters Bern had written were extremely brief. I didn't dislike what I heard, because there was nothing yet to like or dislike—he hadn't got started, really, however much he wanted to think otherwise. Listening to what he read was like being led into a dark hole to see by torch-light the first Malamud story ever scratched upon a cave wall.

I didn't want to lie to him but, looking at those few typewritten pages shaking in his frail hands, I couldn't tell the truth, even if he was expecting it. Only a little evasively, I said that it seemed to me a beginning like all beginnings. That was truthful enough for a man of seventy-one who had published some of the most original works of fiction written by an American in my lifetime. Trying to be constructive, I suggested that the narrative opened too slowly and that he might better begin further along, with one of the later chapters. I asked where it was all going. "What comes next?" I said, hoping we could pass on to what it was he had in mind if not yet down on the page.

But he wouldn't let go of what he'd written, at such cost,

as easily as that. Nothing was ever as easy as that, least of all the end of things. In a soft voice suffused with fury, he replied: "What's next isn't the point."

In the silence that followed, he was perhaps as angry at failing to master the need for assurance that he'd so nakedly displayed as he was chagrined with me for having nothing good to say. He wanted to be told that what he had painfully composed while enduring all his burdens was something more than he himself must have known it to be in his heart. He was suffering so, I wished that I could have said it *was* something more and that if I'd said it, he could have believed me.

Before I left for England in the fall I wrote him a note inviting him and Ann to come down to Connecticut the next summer—it was our turn to entertain them. The response that reached me in London some weeks later was pure, laconic Malamudese. They'd be delighted to visit, but, he reminded me, "next summer is next summer."

He died on March 18, 1986, three days before spring.

Pictures by Guston

"One time, in Woodstock," Ross Feld said, "I stood next to Guston in front of some of these canvases. I hadn't seen them before; I didn't really know what to say. For a time, then, there was silence. After a while, Guston took his thumbnail away from his teeth and said, 'People, you know, complain that it's horrifying. As if it's a picnic for me, who has to come in here every day and see them first thing. But what's the alternative? I'm trying to see how much I can stand.'"

—From *Night Studio: A Memoir of Philip Guston* by Musa Mayer

[1989]

I N 1967, sick of life in the New York art world, Philip Guston left his Manhattan studio forever and took up permanent residence with his wife, Musa, in their Woodstock house on Maverick Road, where they had been living off and on for some twenty years. Two years later, I turned my back on New York to hide out in a small furnished house in Woodstock, across town from Philip, whom I didn't know at the time. I was fleeing the publication of *Portnoy's Complaint*. My overnight notoriety as a sexual freak had become difficult to evade in Manhattan, and so I decided to clear out—first for Yaddo, the upstate artists' colony, and then, beginning in the spring of 1969, for that small rented house tucked out of sight midway up a hillside meadow a couple of miles from Woodstock's main street. I lived there with a young woman who was finishing a Ph.D. and who for several years had been renting a tiny cabin, heated by a wood stove, in the mountainside colony of Byrd-cliffe, which some decades earlier had been a primitive hamlet of Woodstock artists. During the day I wrote on a table in the upstairs spare bedroom while she went off to the cabin to work on her dissertation.

Life in the country with a postgraduate student was anything but freakish, and it provided a combination of social seclusion and physical pleasure that, given the illogic of creation, led me to write, over a four-year period, a cluster of uncharacteristically freakish books. My new reputation as a crazed penis was what instigated the fantasy at the heart of *The Breast*, a book about a college professor who turns into a female breast; it had something to do as well with inspiring the farcical legend of homeless alienation in homespun America that evolved into *The Great American Novel*. The more simplehearted my Woodstock satisfactions, the more tempted I was in my work by the excesses of the Grand Guignol. I'd never felt more imaginatively polymorphous than when I would put two deck chairs on the lawn at the end of the day and we'd stretch out to enjoy the twilight view of the southern foothills of the Catskills, for me unpassable Alps through which no disconcerting irrelevancy could pass. I felt refractory and unreachable and freewheeling, and I was dedicated—perversely overdedicated, probably—to shaking off the vast newfound audience whose collective fantasies were not without their own transforming power.

Guston's situation in 1969—the year we met—was very different. At fifty-six, Philip was twenty years older than I and full of the doubt that can beset an artist of consequence in late middle age. He felt he'd exhausted the means that had unlocked him as an abstract painter, and he was bored and disgusted by the skills that had gained him renown. He didn't want to paint like that ever again; he tried to convince himself he shouldn't paint at all. But since nothing but painting could contain his emotional turbulence, let alone begin to deplete his self-mythologizing monomania, renouncing painting would have been tantamount to committing suicide. Although painting monopolized just enough of his despair and his seismic moodiness to make the anxiety of being himself something even he could sometimes laugh at, it never neutralized the nightmares entirely.

It wasn't supposed to. The nightmares were his not to dissipate with paint but, during the ten years before his death, to intensify with paint, to paint into nightmares that were imperishable and never before incarnated in such trashy props. That terror may be all the more bewildering when it is steeped in farce we know from what we ourselves dream and from what has been dreamed for us by Beckett and Kafka. Philip's discovery—akin to theirs, driven by a delight in mundane objects as boldly distended and bluntly depoeticized as theirs—was of the dread that emanates from the most commonplace appurtenances of the world of utter stupidity. The unexalted vision of everyday things that newspaper cartoon strips had impressed upon him when he was growing up in an immigrant Jewish family in California, the American crumminess for which, even in the heyday of his thoughtful lyricism, he always had an intellectual's soft spot, he came to contemplate—in an exercise familiar to lovers of *Molloy* and *The Castle*—as though his life, both as an artist and as a man, depended on it. This popular imagery of a shallow reality Philip imbued with such a weight of personal sorrow and artistic urgency as to shape in painting a new American landscape of terror.

Cut off from New York and living apart from Woodstock's local artists, with whom he had little in common, Philip often felt out of it: isolated, resentful, uninfluential, misplaced. It wasn't the first time that his ruthless focus on his own imperatives had induced a black mood of alienation, nor was he the first American artist embittered by the syndrome. It was as common among the best as it was among the worst—only with the best it was not necessarily a puerile self-drama concocted out of egomaniacal delusion. In many ways it was a perfectly justified response for an artist like Guston, whose brooding, brainy, hypercritical scrutiny of every last aesthetic choice is routinely travestied by the misjudgments and simplifications that support a major reputation.

Philip and his gloom were not inseparable, however. In the company of the few friends he enjoyed and was willing to see, he could be a cordial, unharried host, exuding a captivating spiritual buoyancy unmarked by anguish. In his physical bearing, too, there was a nimble grace touchingly at variance with the bulky torso of the heavy-drinking, somewhat august-looking, white-haired personage into whom darkly, Jewishly, Don Juanishly handsome Guston had been transformed in his fifties. At dinner, wearing those baggy-bottomed, low-slung khaki trousers of his, with a white cotton shirt open over his burly chest and the sleeves still turned up from working in the studio, he looked like the Old Guard Israeli politicians in whom imperiousness and informality spring from an unassailable core of confidence. It was impossible around the Guston dining table, sharing the rich pasta that Philip had cooked up with a display of jovial expertise, to detect any sign of a self-flagellating component within his prodigious endowment of self-belief. Only in his eyes might you be able to gauge the toll of the wearing oscillation—from iron resolve through rapturous equilibrium to suicidal hopelessness—that underlay a day in the studio.

What caused our friendship to flourish was, to begin with, a similar intellectual outlook, a love for many of the same books as well as a shared delight in what Guston called "crapola," starting with billboards, garages, diners, burger joints, junk shops, auto body shops—all the roadside stuff that we occasionally set out to Kingston to enjoy—and extending from the flat-footed straight talk of the Catskill citizenry to the Uriah Heepisms of our perspiring president. What sealed the camaraderie was that we liked each other's new work. The dissimilarities in our personal lives and our professional fortunes did not obscure the coincidence of our having recently undertaken comparable self-critiques. Independently, impelled by very different dilemmas, each of us had begun to consider crapola not only as a curious subject with strong suggestive powers to which we had a native affinity but as potentially a tool in itself: a blunt aesthetic instrument providing access to a style of representation free of the complexity we were accustomed to valuing. What this self-subversion might be made to yield was anybody's guess, and premonitions of failure couldn't be entirely curbed by the liberating feeling that an artistic about-face usually inspires, at least in the early stages of not quite knowing what you are doing.

At just about the time that I began not quite to know what I was doing exulting in Nixon's lies, or traveling up to Cooperstown's Hall of Fame to immerse myself in baseball lore, or taking seriously the idea of turning a man like myself into a breast—and reading up on endocrinology and mammary glands—Philip was beginning not quite to know what he was doing hanging cartoon light bulbs over the pointed hoods of slit-eyed, cigar-smoking Klansmen painting self-portraits in hideaways cluttered with shoes and clocks and steam irons of the sort that Mutt and Jeff would have been at home with.

Philip's illustrations of incidents in *The Breast,* drawn on ordinary typing paper, were presented to me one evening at dinner shortly after the book's publication. A couple of

years earlier, while I was writing *Our Gang,* Philip had responded to the chapters that I showed him in manuscript with a series of caricatures of Nixon, Kissinger, Agnew, and John Mitchell. He worked on these caricatures with more concentration than he did on the drawings for *The Breast,* and he even toyed with the thought of publishing them as a collection under the title *Poor Richard.* The eight drawings inspired by *The Breast* were simply a spontaneous rejoinder to something he'd liked. The drawings were intended to do nothing other than please me—and did they!

For me his blubbery cartoon rendering of the breast into which Professor David Kepesh is inexplicably transformed —his vision of afflicted Kepesh as a beached mammary groping for contact through a nipple that is an unostentatious amalgam of lumpish, dumb penis and inquisitive nose—managed to encapsulate all the loneliness of Kepesh's humiliation while at the same time adhering to the mordantly comic perspective with which Kepesh tries to view his horrible metamorphosis. Though these drawings were no more than a pleasant diversion for Philip, his predilection for the self-satirization of personal misery (the strategy for effacing the romance of self-pity that stuns us in Gogol's "Diary of a Madman" and "The Nose") as strongly determines the images here as it does in those paintings where his own tiresome addictions and sad renunciations are represented by whiskey bottles and cigarette butts and forlorn insomniacs epically cartoonized. He may only have been playing around, but what he was playing with was the point of view with which he had set about in his studio to overturn his history as a painter and to depict, without rhetorical hedging, the facts of his anxiety as a man. Coincidentally, Philip, who died in 1980 at the age of sixty-six, represents himself in his last paintings as someone who also endured a grotesque transformation— not into a thinking, dismembered sexual gland but into a bloated, cyclopsian, brutish head that has itself been cut loose from the body of its sex.

Rereading Saul Bellow

[2000]

The Adventures of Augie March (1953)

THE TRANSFORMATION of the novelist who published *Dangling Man* in 1944 and *The Victim* in 1947 into the novelist who published *The Adventures of Augie March* in '53 is revolutionary. Bellow overthrows everything: compositional choices grounded in narrative principles of harmony and order, a novelistic ethos indebted to Kafka's *The Trial* and Dostoyevsky's *The Double* and *The Eternal Husband,* as well as a moral perspective that can hardly be said to derive from delight in the flash, color, and plenty of existence. In *Augie March,* a very grand, assertive, freewheeling conception of both the novel and the world the novel represents breaks loose from all sorts of self-imposed strictures, the beginner's principles of composition are subverted, and, like the character of five Properties in *Augie March,* the writer is himself "hipped on superabundance." The pervasive threat that organized the outlook of the hero and the action of the novel in *The Victim* and *Dangling Man* disappears, and the bottled-up aggression that was *The Victim's* Asa Leventhal and the obstructed will that was Joseph in *Dangling Man* emerge as voracious appetite. There is the narcissistic enthusiasm for life in all its hybrid forms propelling Augie March, and there is an inexhaustible passion for a teemingness of dazzling specifics driving Saul Bellow.

The scale dramatically enlarges: the world inflates, and those inhabiting it, monumental, overwhelming, ambitious, energetic people, do not easily, in Augie's words, get "stamped out in the life struggle." The intricate landscape of physical being and the power-seeking of influential personalities make "character" in all its manifestations—particularly its ability indelibly to imprint its presence—less an aspect of the novel than its preoccupation.

Think of Einhorn at the whorehouse, Thea with the eagle, Dingbat and his fighter, Simon coarsely splendid at the Magnuses and violent at the lumberyard. From Chicago to Mexico and the mid-Atlantic and back, it's all Brobdingnag to Augie, observed, however, not by a caustic, angry Swift but by a word-painting Hieronymus Bosch, an American Bosch, an unsermonizing and optimistic Bosch, who detects even in the eeliest slipperiness of his creatures, in their most colossal finagling and conspiring and deceit, what is humanly enrapturing. The intrigues of mankind no longer incite paranoid fear in the Bellow hero but light him up. That the richly rendered surface is manifold with contradiction and ambiguity ceases to be a source of consternation; instead, the "mixed character" of everything is bracing. Manifoldness is fun.

Engorged sentences had existed before in American fiction—notably in Melville and Faulkner—but not quite like those in *Augie March,* which strike me as more than liberty-taking; when mere liberty-taking is driving a writer, it can easily lead to the empty flamboyance of some of *Augie March*'s imitators. I read Bellow's liberty-taking prose as the syntactical demonstration of Augie's large, robust ego, that attentive ego roving and evolving, always in motion, alternately mastered by the force of others and escaping from it. There are sentences in the book whose effervescence, whose undercurrent of buoyancy leave one with the sense of so much going on, a theatrical, exhibitionistic, ardent prose tangle that lets in the dynamism of living without driving mentalness out. This voice no longer encountering resistance is permeated by mind while connected also to the mysteries of feeling. It's a voice unbridled and intelligent both, going at full force and yet always sharp enough to sensibly size things up.

Chapter XVI of *Augie March* is about the attempt, by Thea Fenchel, Augie's headstrong beloved, to train her eagle, Caligula, to attack and capture the large lizards crawling around the mountains outside Acatla, in central Mexico, to make that "menace falling fast from the sky" fit into her scheme of things. It's a chapter of prodigious strength, sixteen bold pages about a distinctly human happening whose mythic aura (and comedy too) is comparable to the great scenes in Faulkner—in *The Bear,* in *Spotted Horses,* in *As I Lay Dying,* throughout *The Wild Palms*—where human resolve pits itself against natural wildness. The combat between Caligula and Thea (for the eagle's body and soul), the wonderfully precise passages describing the eagle soaring off to satisfy his beautiful fiendish trainer and miserably failing her, crystallize a notion about the will to power and dominance that is central to nearly every one of Augie's adventures. "To tell the truth," Augie says near the end of the book, "I'm good and tired of all these big personalities, destiny molders, and heavy-water brains, Machiavellis and wizard evildoers, big-wheels and imposers-upon, absolutists."

On the book's memorable first page, in the second sentence, Augie quotes Heraclitus: a man's character is his fate. But doesn't *The Adventures of Augie March* suggest exactly the opposite, that a man's fate (at least this man's, this Chicago-born Augie's) is the impinging character of others?

Bellow once told me that "somewhere in my Jewish and immigrant blood there were conspicuous traces of doubt as to whether I had the right to practice the writer's trade." He suggested that, at least in part, this doubt permeated his blood because "our own Wasp establishment, represented mainly by Harvard-trained professors," considered a son of immigrant Jews unfit to write books in English. These guys infuriated him.

It may well have been the precious gift of an appropriate fury that launched him into beginning his third book not with the words "I am a Jew, the son of immigrants" but, rather, by warranting that son of immigrant Jews who is Augie March to break the ice with the Harvard-trained professors (as well as everyone else) by flatly decreeing, without apology or hyphenation, "I am an American, Chicago born."

Opening *Augie March* with those six words demonstrates the same sort of assertive gusto that the musical sons of immigrant Jews—Irving Berlin, Aaron Copland, George Gershwin, Ira Gershwin, Richard Rodgers, Lorenz Hart, Jerome Kern, Leonard Bernstein—brought to America's radios, theaters, and concert halls by staking their claim to America (as subject, as inspiration, as audience) in songs like "God Bless America," "This Is the Army, Mr. Jones," "Oh, How I Hate to Get Up in the Morning," "Manhattan," and "Ol' Man River"; in musical plays like *Oklahoma!, West Side Story, Porgy and Bess, On the Town, Show Boat, Annie Get Your Gun,* and *Of Thee I Sing;* in ballet music like *Appalachian Spring, Rodeo,* and *Billy the Kid.* Back in the teens, when the immigration was still going on, back in the twenties, the thirties, the forties, even into the fifties, none of these American-raised boys whose parents or grandparents had spoken Yiddish had the slightest interest in writing shtetl kitsch such as came along in the sixties with *Fiddler on the Roof.* Having themselves been freed by their families' emigration from the pious orthodoxy and the social authoritarianism that were such a great source of shtetl claustrophobia, why would they want to? In secular, democratic, unclaustrophobic America, Augie will, as he says, "go at things as I have taught myself, free-style."

This assertion of unequivocal, unquellable citizenship in free-style America (and the five-hundred-odd-page book that followed) was precisely the bold stroke required to abolish anyone's doubts about the American writing credentials of an immigrant son like Saul Bellow. Augie, at the very end of his book, exuberantly cries out, "Look at me, going everywhere! Why, I am a sort of Columbus of those near-at-hand." Going where his pedigreed betters wouldn't have believed he had any right to go with the American language, Bellow was indeed Columbus for people like me, the grandchildren of immigrants, who set out as American writers after him.

Seize the Day (1956)

THREE YEARS after *The Adventures of Augie March* appeared, Bellow published *Seize the Day*, a short novel that is the fictional antithesis of *Augie March*. In form spare and compact and tightly organized, it is a sorrow-filled book, set in a hotel for the aged on the Upper West Side of Manhattan, a book populated largely by people old, sick, and dying, while *Augie March* is a vast, sprawling, loquacious book, spilling over with everything, including authorial high spirits, and set wherever life's fullness can be rapturously perceived. *Seize the Day* depicts the culmination, in a single day, of the breakdown of a man who is the opposite of Augie March in every important way. Where Augie is the opportunity seizer, a fatherless slum kid eminently adoptable, Tommy Wilhelm is the mistake maker with a prosperous old father who is very much present but who wants nothing to do with him and his problems. Inasmuch as Tommy's father is characterized in the book, it is through his relentless distaste for his son. Tommy is brutally disowned, eminently unadoptable, largely because he is bereft of the lavish endowment of self-belief, verve, and vibrant adventurousness that is Augie's charm. Where Augie's is an ego triumphantly buoyed up and swept along by the strong currents of life, Tommy's is an ego quashed beneath its burden— Tommy is "assigned to be the carrier of a load which was his own self, his characteristic self." The ego roar amplified by *Augie March*'s prose exuberance Augie joyously articulates on the book's final page: "Look at me, going everywhere!" *Look at me*—the vigorous, child's demand for attention, the cry of exhibitionistic confidence.

The cry resounding through *Seize the Day* is *Help me*. In vain Tommy utters, Help me, help me, I'm getting nowhere, and not only to his own father, Dr. Adler, but to all the false, rogue fathers who succeed Dr. Adler and to whom Tommy foolishly entrusts his hope, his money, or both. Augie is adopted left and right, people rush to support him and dress him, to educate and transform him. Augie's need is to accumulate vivid and flamboyant patron-admirers while Tommy's pathos is to amass mistakes: "Maybe the making of mistakes expressed the very purpose of his life and the essence of his being here." Tommy, at forty-four, searches desperately for a parent, any parent, to rescue him from imminent destruction, while Augie is already a larkily independent escape artist at twenty-two.

Speaking of his own past, Bellow once said, "It has been a lifelong pattern with me to come back to strength from a position of extreme weakness." Does his history of oscillation from the abyss to the peak and back again find a literary analogue in the dialectical relationship of these two consecutive books of the 1950s? Was the claustrophobic chronicle of failure that is *Seize the Day* undertaken as a grim corrective to the fervor informing its irrepressible predecessor, as the antidote to *Augie March*'s manic openness? By writing *Seize the Day*, Bellow seems to have been harking back (if not deliberately, perhaps just reflexively) to the ethos of *The Victim*, to a dour pre-Augie world where the hero under scrutiny is threatened by enemies, overwhelmed by uncertainty, stalled by confusion, held in check by grievance.

Henderson the Rain King (1959)

ONLY SIX YEARS after *Augie,* and there he is again, breaking loose. But whereas with *Augie* he jettisons the conventions of his first two, "proper" books, with *Henderson the Rain*

King he delivers himself from *Augie,* a book in no way proper. The exotic locale, the volcanic hero, the comic calamity that is his life, the inner turmoil of perpetual yearning, the magical craving quest, the mythical (Reichian?) regeneration through the great wet gush of the blocked-up stuff—all brand-new.

To yoke together two mighty dissimilar endeavors: Bellow's Africa operates for Henderson as Kafka's castle village does for K., affording the perfect unknown testing ground for the alien hero to actualize the deepest, most ineradicable of his needs—to burst his "spirit's sleep," if he can, through the intensity of useful labor. "I want," that objectless, elemental cri de coeur, could as easily have been K.'s as Eugene Henderson's. There all similarity ends, to be sure. Unlike the Kafkean man endlessly obstructed from achieving his desire, Henderson is the undirected human force whose raging insistence miraculously *does* get through. K. is an initial, with the biographylessness—and the pathos—that that implies, while Henderson's biography weighs a ton. A boozer, a giant, a Gentile, a middle-aged multimillionaire in a state of continual emotional upheaval, Henderson is hemmed in by the disorderly chaos of "my parents, my wives, my girls, my children, my farm, my animals, my habits, my money, my music lessons, my drunkenness, my prejudices, my brutality, my teeth, my face, my soul!" Because of all his deformities and mistakes, Henderson, in his own thinking, is as much a disease as he is a man. He takes leave of home (rather like the author who is imagining him) for a continent peopled by tribal blacks who turn out to be his very cure. Africa as medicine. Henderson the Remedy Maker.

Brilliantly funny, all new, a second enormous emancipation, a book that wants to be serious and unserious at the same time (and is), a book that invites an academic reading while ridiculing such a reading and sending it up, a stunt of a book, but a sincere stunt—a screwball book, but not without great screwball authority.

Herzog (1964)

THE CHARACTER of Moses Herzog, that labyrinth of contradiction and self-division—the wild man and the earnest person with a "Biblical sense of personal experience" and an innocence as phenomenal as his sophistication, intense yet passive, reflective yet impulsive, sane yet insane, emotional, complicated, an expert on pain vibrant with feeling and yet disarmingly simple, a clown in his vengeance and rage, a fool in whom hatred breeds comedy, a sage and knowing scholar in a treacherous world, yet still adrift in the great pool of childhood love, trust, and excitement in things (and hopelessly attached to this condition), an aging lover of enormous vanity and narcissism with a lovingly harsh attitude toward himself, whirling in the wash cycle of a rather generous self-awareness while at the same time aesthetically attracted to anyone vivid, overpoweringly drawn to bullies and bosses, to theatrical know-it-alls, lured by their seeming certainty and by the raw authority of their unambiguity, feeding on their intensity until he's all but crushed by it—this Herzog is Bellow's grandest creation, American literature's Leopold Bloom, except with a difference: in *Ulysses*, the encyclopedic mind of the author is transmuted into the linguistic flesh of the novel, and Joyce never cedes to Bloom his own great erudition, intellect, and breadth of rhetoric, whereas in *Herzog* Bellow endows his hero with all of that, not only with a state of mind and a cast of mind but with a mind that *is* a mind.

It's a mind rich and wide-ranging but turbulent with troubles, bursting, swarming with grievance and indignation, a bewildered mind that, in the first sentence of the book, openly, with good reason, questions its equilibrium, and not in highbrowese but in the classic vernacular formulation: "If I am out of my mind . . ." This mind, so forceful, so tenacious, overstocked with the best that has been thought and said, a mind elegantly turning out the most informed generalizations about a lot of the world and its history, happens also to suspect its most fundamental power, the very capacity for comprehension.

The axis on which the book's adulterous drama turns, the scene that sends Herzog racing off to Chicago to pick up a loaded pistol to kill Madeleine and Gersbach and instead initiates his final undoing, takes place in a New York courtroom, where Herzog, loitering while waiting for his lawyer to show up, comes upon the nightmare-parody version of his own suffering. It is the trial of a hapless, degraded mother who, with her degenerate lover, has murdered her own little child. So overcome with horror is Herzog at what he sees and hears that he is prompted to cry out to himself, "I fail to understand!"—familiar-enough everyday words, but for Herzog a humbling, pain-ridden, reverberating admission that dramatically connects the intricate wickerwork of his mental existence to the tormenting grid of error and disappointment that is his personal life. Since for Herzog understanding is an impediment to instinctive force, it is when understanding fails him that he reaches for a gun (the very one with which his own father once clumsily threatened to kill *him*)—though, in the end, being Herzog, he cannot fire it. Being Herzog (and his angry father's angry son), he finds firing the pistol "nothing but a thought."

But if Herzog fails to understand, who *does* understand, and what is all this thinking *for*? Why all this uninhibited reflection in Bellow's books in the first place? I don't mean the uninhibited reflection of characters like Tamkin in *Seize the Day*, or even King Dahfu in *Henderson*, who seem to dish out their spoof wisdom as much for Bellow to have the fun of inventing it as to create a second realm of confusion in the minds of heroes already plenty confused on their own. I'm referring, rather, to the nearly impossible undertaking that marks Bellow's work as strongly as it does the novels of Robert Musil and Thomas Mann: the struggle not only to infuse fiction with mind but to make mentalness itself central to the hero's dilemma—to think, in books like *Herzog*, about the *problem* of thinking.

Now, Bellow's special appeal, and not just to me, is that in his characteristically American way he has managed brilliantly to close the gap between Thomas Mann and Damon Runyon, but that doesn't minimize the scope of what, beginning with *Augie March*, he so ambitiously set out to do: to bring into play (into *free* play) the intellectual faculties that, in writers like Mann, Musil, and him, are no less engaged by the spectacle of life than by the mind's imaginative component, to make rumination congruent with what is represented, to hoist the author's thinking up from the depths to the narrative's surface without sinking the narrative's mimetic power, without the book's superficially meditating on itself, without making a transparently ideological claim on the reader, and without imparting wisdom, as do Tamkin and King Dahfu, flatly unproblematized.

Herzog is Bellow's first protracted expedition as a writer into the immense domain of sex. Herzog's women are of the greatest importance to him, exciting his vanity, arousing his carnality, channeling his love, drawing his curiosity, and, by registering his cleverness, charm, and good looks, feeding in the man the joys of a boy—in their adoration is his validation. With every insult they hurl and every epithet they coin, with each fetching turn of the head, comforting touch of the hand, angry twist of the mouth, his women fascinate Herzog with that human otherness that so overpowers him in *both* sexes. But it is the women especially—until the final pages, that is, when Herzog turns away from his Berkshires retreat even well-meaning Ramona and the generous pleasures of the seraglio that are her specialty, when he at long last emancipates himself from the care of another woman, even this most gentle fondler of them all, and, so as to repair himself, undertakes what is for him the heroic project of living alone, shedding the women and, shedding with them, of all things, the explaining, the justifying, the thinking, divesting himself, if only temporarily, of the all-encompassing and habitual sources of his pleasure and misery—it is the women especially who bring out the portraitist in Herzog, a multitalented painter who can be as lavish in describing the generous mistress as Renoir; as tender in presenting the adorable daughter as Degas; as compassionate, as respectful of age, as knowledgeable of hardship in picturing the ancient stepmother—or his own dear mother in her slavish immigrant misery—as Rembrandt; as devilish, finally, as Daumier in depicting the adulterous wife who discerns, in Herzog's loving and scheming best friend, Valentine Gersbach, her crudely theatrical equal.

In all of literature, I know of no more emotionally susceptible male, of no man who brings a greater focus or intensity to his engagement with women than this Herzog,

who collects them both as an adoring suitor and as a husband—a cuckolded husband getting a royal screwing who,
in the grandeur of his jealous rage and in the naiveté of his
blind uxoriousness, is a kind of comic-strip amalgam of
General Othello and Charles Bovary. Anyone wishing to
have some fun in retelling *Madame Bovary* from Charles's
perspective, or *Anna Karenina* from Karenin's, will find in
Herzog the perfect how-to book. (Not that one easily envi-
sions Karenin, à la Herzog with Gersbach, handing over to
Vronsky Anna's diaphragm.)

Herzog lays claim to being a richer novel even than *Augie
March* because Bellow's taking on board, for the first time,
the full sexual cargo allows for a brand of suffering to pen-
etrate his fictional world that was largely precluded from
Augie and *Henderson*. It turns out that even more is unlocked in the Bellow hero by suffering than by euphoria.
How much more credible, how much more important he
becomes when the male wound, in its festering enormity,
ravages the euphoric appetite for "the rich life-cake," and
the vulnerability to humiliation, betrayal, melancholy, fatigue, loss, paranoia, obsession, and despair is revealed to
be so sweeping that neither an Augie's relentless optimism nor a Henderson's mythical giantism can stave off
any longer the truth about pain. Once Bellow grafts onto
Henderson's intensity—and onto Augie March's taste for
grandiose types and dramatic encounters—Tommy Wilhelm's condition of helplessness, he puts the whole Bellovian symphony in play, with its lushly comical orchestration
of misery.

In *Herzog*, there is no sustained chronological action—
there's barely *any* action—that takes place outside Herzog's

brain. It isn't that, as a storyteller, Bellow apes Faulkner in *The Sound and the Fury* or Virginia Woolf in *The Waves*. The long, shifting, fragmented interior monologue of *Herzog* seems to have more in common with Gogol's "Diary of a Madman," where the disjointed perception is dictated by the mental state of the central character rather than by an author's impatience with traditional means of narration. What makes Gogol's madman mad, however, and Bellow's sane, is that Gogol's madman, incapable of overhearing himself, is unfortified by the spontaneous current of irony and parody that ripples through Herzog's every thought— even when Herzog is most bewildered—and that is inseparable from his take on himself and his disaster, however excruciating his pain.

In the Gogol story, the madman obtains a bundle of letters written by a dog, the pet belonging to the young woman of whom he is hopelessly (insanely) enamored. Feverishly, he sits down to read every word the brilliant dog has written, searching for any reference to himself. In *Herzog*, Bellow goes Gogol one better: the brilliant dog who writes the letters is Herzog. Letters to his dead mother, to his living mistress, to his first wife, to President Eisenhower, to Chicago's police commissioner, to Adlai Stevenson, to Nietzsche ("My dear sir, May I ask a question from the floor?"), to Teilhard de Chardin ("Dear Father . . . Is the carbon molecule lined with thought?"), to Heidegger ("Dear Doktor Professor . . . I should like to know what you mean by the expression 'the fall into the quotidian.' When did this fall occur? Where were we standing when it happened?"), to the credit department of Marshall Field & Co. ("I am no longer responsible for the debts of Madeleine P. Herzog"), even, in the end, a letter to God ("How my mind has struggled to make coherent sense. I have not been too good at it. But have desired to do your unknowable will, taking it, and you, without symbols. Everything of intensest significance. Especially if divested of me").

This book of a thousand delights offers no greater delight than those letters, and no better key with which to both unlock Herzog's remarkable intelligence and enter into the depths of his turmoil over the wreckage of his life. The letters are his intensity demonstrated; they provide the stage for his intellectual theater, the one-man show where he is least likely to act the role of the fool.

Mr. Sammler's Planet (1970)

"IS OUR SPECIES CRAZY?" A Swiftian question. A Swiftian note as well in the laconic Sammlerian reply: "Plenty of evidence."

Reading *Mr. Sammler's Planet*, I am reminded of *Gulliver's Travels:* by the overwhelming estrangement of the hero from the New York of the 1960s; by the rebuke he, with his history, embodies to the human status of those whose "sexual madness" he must witness; by his Gulliverian obsession with human physicality, human biology, the almost mythic distaste evoked in him by the body, its appearance, its functions, its urges, its pleasures, its secretions and smells. Then there's the preoccupation with the radical vincibility of one's physical being. As a frail, displaced refugee of the Holocaust horror, as one who escaped miraculously from the Nazi slaughter, who rose, with but one eye, from a pile of Jewish bodies left for dead by a German extermination squad, Mr. Sammler registers that most disorienting of blows to civic confidence—the disappearance, in a great city, of security, of safety, and, with that, the burgeoning among the vulnerable of fear-ridden, alienating paranoia.

For it is fear as well as disgust that vitiates Sammler's faith in the species and threatens his tolerance even for those closest to him—fear of "the soul . . . in this vehemence . . . the extremism and fanaticism of human nature." Having moved beyond the Crusoe-adventurousness of ebullient Augie and Henderson to delineate, as dark farce, the marital betrayal of the uncomprehending genius Herzog, Bellow next opens out his contemplative imagination to one of the greatest betrayals of all, at least as perceived by the refugee-victim Sammler in his Swiftian revulsion with the sixties: the betrayal by the crazy species of the civilized ideal.

Herzog, during his most searing moment of suffering, admits to himself, "I fail to understand!" But, despite old Sammler's Oxonian reserve and cultivated detachment, at the climax of *his* adventure—with license, disorder, and lawlessness within the network of his vividly eccentric family and beyond them, in New York's streets, subways, buses, shops, and college classrooms—the admission that is wrung from him (and that, for me, stands as the motto of this book) is far more shattering: "I am horrified!"

The triumph of *Mr. Sammler's Planet* is the invention of Sammler, with the credentials that accrue to him through his European education—his history of suffering history, and his Nazi-blinded eye—as "the registrar of madness." The juxtaposition of the personal plight of the protagonist with the particulars of the social forces he encounters, the resounding, ironic rightness of that juxtaposition, accounts for the impact here, as it does in every memorable fiction.

Sammler, sharply set apart by his condition of defenseless dignity, strikes me as the perfect instrument to receive anything in society at all bizarre or menacing, the historical victim abundantly qualified by experience to tellingly provide a harsh, hardened twentieth-century perspective on "mankind in a revolutionary condition."

I wonder which came first in the book's development, the madness or the registrar, Sammler or the sixties.

Humboldt's Gift (1975)

Humboldt's Gift is far and away the screwiest of the euphoric going-every-which-way out-and-out comic novels, the books that materialize at the very tip-top of the Bellovian mood swing, the merry music of the egosphere that is *Augie March, Henderson,* and *Humboldt* and that Bellow emits more or less periodically, between his burrowings through the dark down-in-the-dumps novels, such as *The Victim, Seize the Day, Mr. Sammler's Planet,* and *The Dean's December,* where the bewildering pain issuing from the heroes' wounds is not taken lightly either by them or by Bellow. (*Herzog* strikes me as supreme among Bellow's novels for its magical integration of this characteristic divergence. If one wished to play literary chef and turn *Humboldt's Gift* into *Herzog,* the simple recipe might go as follows: first, cut away and set aside Humboldt; next, extract from Humboldt his mad suffering and bind it to Citrine's reflective brilliance; last, toss in Gersbach—and there's your book. It's Gersbach's betrayal that stirs up in Herzog the murderous paranoia that is excited in Humboldt by, among others, Citrine!)

Humboldt is the screwiest, by which I also mean the most

brazen of the comedies, loopier and more carnivalesque than the others, Bellow's only joyously open libidinous book and, rightly, the most recklessly crossbred fusion of disparate strains, and for a paradoxically compelling reason: Citrine's terror. Of what? Of mortality, of having to meet (regardless of his success and his great eminence) Humboldt's fate. Underlying the book's buoyant engagement with the scrambling, gorging, thieving, hating, and destroying of Charlie Citrine's on-the-make world, underlying everything, including the centrifugal manner of the book's telling—and exposed directly enough in Citrine's eagerness to metabolize the extinction-defying challenge of Rudolf Steiner's anthroposophy—is his terror of dying. What's disorienting Citrine happens also to be what's blowing narrative decorum to kingdom come: the panicky dread of oblivion, the old-fashioned garden-variety Everyman horror of death.

"How sad," says Citrine, "about all this human nonsense which keeps us from the large truth." But the human nonsense is what he loves and loves to recount and what delights him most about being alive. Again: "When . . . would I rise . . . above all . . . the wastefully and randomly human . . . to enter higher worlds?" Higher worlds? Where would Citrine be—where would *Bellow* be—without the randomly human driving the superdrama of the *lower* world, the elemental superdrama that is the worldly desire for fame (as exhibited by Von Humboldt Fleisher, the luckless, mentally unsound counterpart of fortunate, sane Citrine—Humboldt, who wishes both to be spiritual and to make it big, and whose nightmare failure is the flip-side travesty of Citrine's success), for money (Humboldt, Thaxter, Denise, plus Renata's mother the Señora, plus Citrine's brother Julius, plus more or less everyone else), for revenge (Denise, Cantabile), for esteem (Humboldt, Cantabile, Thaxter, Citrine), for the hottest of hot sex (Citrine, Renata, et al.), not to mention that worldliest of worldly desires, Citrine's own, the hellbent lusting after life eternal?

Why does Citrine wish so feverishly never to leave here if not for this laugh-a-minute immersion in the violence and the turbulence of the clownish greediness that he disparagingly calls "the moronic inferno"? "Some people," he says, "are so actual that they beat down my critical powers." And beat down any desire to exchange even the connection to their viciousness for the serenity of the everlasting. Where but the moronic inferno could his "complicated subjectivity" have so much to take in? Out in some vaporous Zip Codeless noplace, nostalgically swapping moronic-inferno stories with the shade of Rudolf Steiner?

And isn't it something like the same moronic inferno that Charlie Citrine excitedly memorializes as it rages in the streets, courtrooms, bedrooms, restaurants, sweat baths, and office buildings of Chicago that so sickens Artur Sammler in its diabolic 1960s-Manhattan incarnation? *Humboldt's Gift* seems like the enlivening tonic Bellow brewed to recover from the sorrowful grieving and moral suffering of *Mr. Sammler's Planet*. It's Bellow's cheerful version of Ecclesiastes: all is vanity and isn't it something!

What's He in Chicago For?

HUMBOLDT ON Citrine (my edition page 2): "After making this dough why does he bury himself in the sticks? What's he in Chicago for?"

Citrine on himself (page 63): "My mind was in one of its Chicago states. How should I describe this phenomenon?"

Citrine on being a Chicagoan (page 95): "I could feel the need to laugh rising, mounting, always a sign that my weakness for the sensational, my American, Chicagoan (as well as personal) craving for high stimuli, for incongruities and extremes, was aroused."

And (further along on page 95): "Such information about corruption, if you had grown up in Chicago, was easy to accept. It even satisfied a certain need. It harmonized with one's Chicago view of society."

On the other hand, there's Citrine's being out of place in Chicago (page 225): "In Chicago my personal aims were bunk, my outlook a foreign ideology." And (page 251): "It was now apparent to me that I was neither of Chicago nor sufficiently beyond it, and that Chicago's material and daily interests and phenomena were neither actual and vivid enough nor symbolically clear enough to me."

Keeping in mind these remarks—and there are many more like them throughout *Humboldt's Gift*—look back to the 1940s and observe that Bellow started off as a writer *without* Chicago's organizing his idea of himself the way it does Charlie Citrine's. Yes, a few Chicago streets are occasionally sketched in as the backdrop to *Dangling Man,* but, aside from darkening the pervasive atmosphere of gloom, Chicago seems a place that is almost foreign to the hero; certainly it is alien to him. *Dangling Man* is not a book about a man in a city; it's about a mind in a room. Not until the third book, *Augie March,* did Bellow fully apprehend Chicago as that valuable hunk of literary property, that tangible, engrossing American place that was his to claim as commandingly as Sicily was monopolized by Verga, London by Dickens, and the Mississippi River by Mark Twain. It's with a comparable tentativeness or wariness that Faulkner (the other of America's two greatest twentieth-century novelist-regionalists) came to imaginative ownership of Lafayette County, Mississippi. Faulkner situated his first book, *Soldier's Pay* (1926), in Georgia, his second, *Mosquitoes* (1927), in New Orleans, and it was only with the masterly burst of *Sartoris, The Sound and the Fury,* and *As I Lay Dying,* in 1929–30, that he found—as did Bellow after taking *his* first, impromptu geographical steps—the location to engender those human struggles which, in turn, would fire up his intensity and provoke that impassioned response to a place and its history which at times propels Faulkner's sentences to the brink of unintelligibility and even beyond.

I wonder if at the outset Bellow shied away from seizing Chicago as his because he didn't want to be known as a Chicago writer, any more, perhaps, than he wanted to be known as a Jewish writer. Yes, you're from Chicago, and of course you're a Jew—but how these things are going to figure in your work, or if they should figure at all, isn't easy to puzzle out right off. Besides, you have other ambitions, inspired by your European masters, by Dostoyevsky, Gogol, Proust, Kafka, and such ambitions don't include writing about the neighbors gabbing on the back porch . . . Does this line of thought in any way resemble Bellow's before he finally laid claim to the immediate locale?

Of course, after *Augie* it was some ten years before, in *Herzog,* Bellow took on Chicago in a big way again. Ever since then, the distinctly "Chicago view" has been of recurring interest to him, especially when the city provides, as in

Humboldt, a contrast of comically illuminating proportions between "the open life which is elementary, easy for everyone to read, and characteristic of this place, Chicago, Illinois" and the reflective bent of the preoccupied hero. This combat, vigorously explored, is at the heart of *Humboldt,* as it is of Bellow's next novel, *The Dean's December* (1982). Here, however, the exploration is not comic but rancorous. The mood darkens, the depravity deepens, and under the pressure of violent racial antagonisms, Chicago, Illinois, becomes demoniacal: "On his own turf . . . he found a wilderness wilder than the Guiana bush . . . desolation . . . endless square miles of ruin . . . wounds, lesions, cancers, destructive fury, death . . . the terrible wildness and dread in this huge place."

The book's very point is that this huge place is Bellow's no longer. Nor is it Augie's, Herzog's, or Citrine's. By the time he comes to write *The Dean's December,* some thirty years after *Augie March,* his hero, Dean Corde, has become the city's Sammler.

What is he in Chicago for? This Chicagoan in pain no longer knows. Bellow is banished.

Also available in Vintage

Philip Roth

AMERICAN PASTORAL

'Brilliantly written...angry, grieving, witty, acute...
compellingly and convincingly rendered'
Sunday Times

Seymour 'Swede' Levov – a legendary high school athlete,
a devoted family man, a hard worker, the prosperous
inheritor of his father's Newark glove factory – comes of
age in thriving, triumphant post-war America. But everything he loves is lost when the country begins to run amok
in the turbulent 1960s. *American Pastoral* is the story of a
fortunate American's rise and fall – of a strong, confident
master of social equilibrium overwhelmed by the forces of
social disorder.

'Full of insight, full of sharp ironic twists, full of wisdom
about American idealism, and full of terrific fun...A
profound and personal meditation on the changes in the
American psyche over the last 50 years'
Financial Times

'A tragedy of classical proportions...A magnificent novel'
The Times

VINTAGE

VINTAGE

Also available in Vintage

Philip Roth

PORTNOY'S COMPLAINT

'The most outrageously funny book about sex yet written'
Guardian

The famous confession of Alexander Portnoy, who is thrust
through life by his unappeasable sexuality, yet held back
at the same time by the iron grip of his unforgettable
childhood.

'Roth's gift for fantasy, his superb dialogue, his ability to
evoke places and atmospheres, make *Portnoy's Complaint*
at once hilariously, scabrously funny and deeply moving'
Financial Times

'A hysterically funny monologue which has already added a
new prototype to American literature...Anyone who can
recall anything of the awesome mystery and humiliating
farce of growing up will find this book compulsive reading.
And it is blessedly, extremely funny'
Spectator

VINTAGE